AF306903

Tarek Frikha

Embedded systems design

Tarek Frikha

Embedded systems design

The VHDL language

ScienciaScripts

Imprint

Any brand names and product names mentioned in this book are subject to trademark, brand or patent protection and are trademarks or registered trademarks of their respective holders. The use of brand names, product names, common names, trade names, product descriptions etc. even without a particular marking in this work is in no way to be construed to mean that such names may be regarded as unrestricted in respect of trademark and brand protection legislation and could thus be used by anyone.

Cover image: www.ingimage.com

This book is a translation from the original published under ISBN 978-620-6-70458-4.

Publisher:
Sciencia Scripts
is a trademark of
Dodo Books Indian Ocean Ltd. and OmniScriptum S.R.L publishing group

120 High Road, East Finchley, London, N2 9ED, United Kingdom
Str. Armeneasca 28/1, office 1, Chisinau MD-2012, Republic of Moldova, Europe
Printed at: see last page
ISBN: 978-620-8-07041-0

Copyright © Tarek Frikha
Copyright © 2024 Dodo Books Indian Ocean Ltd. and OmniScriptum S.R.L publishing group

Contents

General introduction

The aim of this course is to describe the VHDL modelling language [1]. VHDL is used to describe the logic structure and function of digital systems at a number of levels of abstraction, from system level to gate level. It is designed, among other things, as a modelling language for specification and simulation. We can also use it for hardware synthesis if we restrict ourselves to a subset that can be automatically translated into hardware.

VHDL was born out of the US government's Very High Speed Integrated Circuits (VHSIC) programme. During this programme, it became clear that a standard language was needed to describe the structure and function of integrated circuits (ICs). This led to the development of the VHSIC hardware description language (VHDL). It was then developed under the auspices of the Institute of Electrical and Electronic Engineers (IEEE)[2] and adopted in the form of IEEE Standard 1076, *Standard VHDL Language Reference Manual,* in 1987. This first standard version of the language is often referred to as VHDL-87.

Like all IEEE standards, the VHDL standard is revised at least every five years. Comments and suggestions from users of the 1987 standard were analysed by the IEEE working group responsible for VHDL and, in 1992, a revised version of the standard was proposed. This was finally adopted in 1993, resulting in VHDL-93. A new revision cycle for the standard began in 1998. This process was completed in 2001, resulting in the current version of the language, VHDL-2002 [3].

This tutorial presents the language features that are common to all versions of the language. They are expressed using the syntax of VHDL-93 and later versions. Some aspects of the syntax are incompatible with the original VHDL-87 version. However, most tools now support at least VHDL-93, so syntax differences should not be a problem [4].

In this document, we will first describe the VHDL design flow. Next, we will describe the fundamental concepts of VHDL. Next, we will highlight the basic VHDL constructs. Finally, we will propose some examples of corrected VHDL architectures.

CHAPTER 1

VHDL design flow.

1. Introduction :

Design flow refers to the sequence of steps involved in transforming an idea, specification or problem into a tangible electronic product. This can include hardware design, software programming, or a combination of both. In the context of hardware design, such as using the VHDL language, the design flow typically follows several key stages. In this chapter we will detail the different stages of the design flow

2. Design flow :

The design flow for implementing a VHDL architecture can be divided into 5 parts. These parts are as follows:

- Editing text or graphics
- VHDL simulation
- VHDL synthesis
- Time extraction
- Placement and routing (P&R)

In the various parts of this chapter, we will detail the different components of this flow. These steps are the foundations for setting up an optimised and functional architecture. Figure 1 shows the different stages of our design flow.

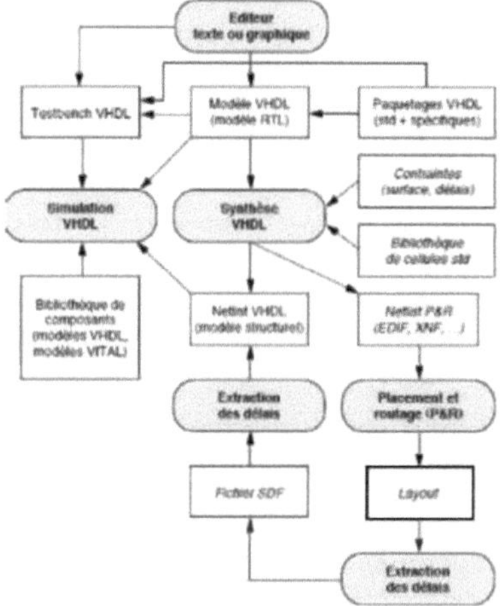

Figure 1 VHDL design flow

3. Text or graphics editor :

VHDL (VHSIC Hardware Description Language), as described in the general introduction, is a hardware description language used to model and design electronic circuits. It offers two complementary approaches to design: writing text-based VHDL code and using graphical editors.

a. CodeVHDLTextual:

In this approach, designers write VHDL code using a standard text editor. The text code describes the behaviour and structure of the circuit to be designed.

The text editor is crucial for writing, organising and editing VHDL code. This editor needs to provide features such as syntax highlighting (highlighting of keywords, operators, etc.), automatic indentation, line numbering, and search tools to make navigating the code easier.

One of the most important advantages of the text-based approach is that it provides a precise and detailed description of the circuit. It offers fine-grained control over the source code, which can be essential for complex projects requiring extensive optimisation and customisation.

b.   Graphic Editor :

The graphical editor is based on certain VHDL design tools. These tools offer graphical editors that allow designers to create schematics of the circuit using a graphical interface. These schematics can then be translated into VHDL code.

The importance of the graphical editor lies in the fact that it simplifies the creation of models by allowing designers to visually represent the structure of the circuit. It provides an intuitive graphical view of the system, which can be particularly useful for understanding and visualising complex circuits.

One of the advantages of the graphical editor is that it can speed up the design process for simple tasks, and it can be more accessible for beginners. It also promotes communication between team members, as the graphical representation is often easier to understand for those unfamiliar with VHDL code.

In short, text-based VHDL code is essential for accurately describing and finely controlling the behaviour of a circuit. The text editor makes it easy to write, modify and manage source code. On the other hand, the graphical editor offers a visual approach, facilitating overall understanding and communication, particularly useful in the initial design phases or for multidisciplinary teams. The two approaches can coexist and be used according to the specific needs of a project.

As a result of preparing the code for our architecture using either the graphical or text editor, we will have two possible outputs: the TestBench or the VHDL model, and more specifically the RTL model.

c.   TestbenchVHDL:

The VHDL testbench [5] is a crucial simulation environment used to verify the behaviour of electronic circuits before they are implemented. It is divided into structural testbenches for testing individual components and system-level testbenches for validating the overall system. These testbenches include elements such as entity instantiation, signal generators, simulation processes, assertions and VHDL simulation tools with waveform viewers. Testbenches are essential for identifying and correcting design errors, ensuring correct circuit functionality and facilitating complete system verification.

d.   VHDL model:

An RTL (Register-Transfer Level) model [6] in VHDL represents the internal behaviour of an electronic circuit by describing data transfers between registers. It specifies operations at a level of description lower than the algorithmic level, but higher than the level of the specific technology. RTL entities define logic modules that interact through signals and registers. This model is crucial for hardware design, providing an abstract representation of circuit operation, facilitating logic synthesis and verification prior to hardware implementation. RTL description in VHDL uses processes to describe sequential behaviour and signal assignments to represent parallel operations.

Other inputs to Testbench and RTL models include VHDL packages. These packages are the result of a set of functions that are brought together to perform a specific process. The packages include logic packages (logic gates, etc.), arithmetic packages (addition, subtraction, etc.) and so on.

4.   VHDL simulation :

VHDL simulation is a crucial step in the electronic circuit design process. It consists of virtually executing the VHDL code in a simulation environment to evaluate the behaviour of the circuit before it is implemented in hardware. VHDL simulators, such as ModelSim [7], VCS or GHDL, are used to run testbenches and verify the functionality of the design. Simulation is used to detect and correct design errors, validate circuit operation under different conditions and analyse the resulting waveforms.

Designers can also use breakpoints, assertions and waveform viewers to debug VHDL code. In this way, VHDL simulation helps to ensure the reliability and performance of the circuit before it is manufactured. Figure 2 shows an example of VHDL code simulation using ModelSim software. Apart from the Testbench and the RTL model, the other blocks used for VHDL Simulation include :

- Component libraries: these are used to simulate certain predefined functions.
- VHDL Netlists: these Netlists can be incorporated for VHDL simulation. It is in this case that Netlists are used.

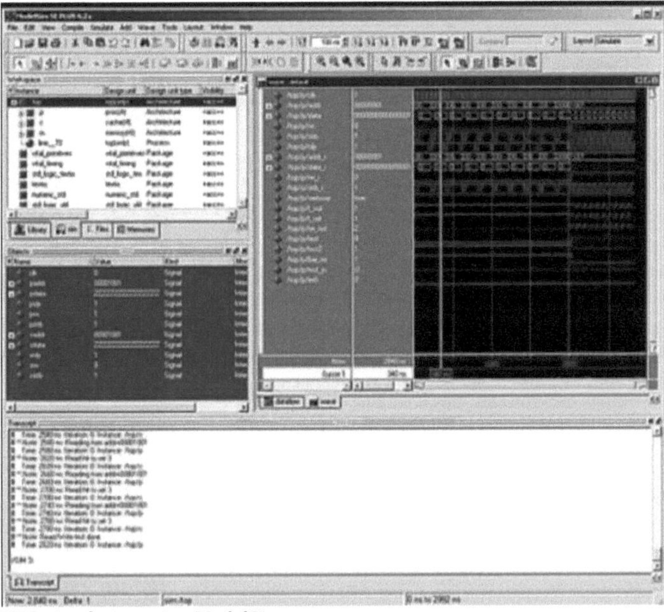

Figure 2 VHDL simulation using ModelSim

5. VHDL synthesis :

VHDL synthesis is the process of converting a hardware description written in VHDL into a Netlist representation, which specifies the logical structure of the circuit in terms of logic gates, flip-flops and other basic elements. This process moves the design from the level of algorithmic abstraction to a lower-level representation suitable for hardware implementation.

Here are some key points about VHDL synthesis:

a. Objective:

The main objective of the synthesis is to transform the behavioural or structural description in VHDL into an equivalent representation that is closer to the hardware.

b. Synthesis tools :

VHDL synthesis tools, such as Synopsys Design Compiler, Xilinx Vivado, or Intel Quartus Prime, analyse the VHDL code and generate a netlist that represents the logical structure of the circuit.

c. Optimisations :

The synthesis tools carry out optimisations to improve circuit performance, reduce energy consumption, minimise the surface area occupied and comply with timing constraints.

d.   Synthesis constraints :

Designers can specify synthesis constraints to guide the process, including timing constraints, power constraints and placement constraints.

e.   Timing analysis :

The synthesis tools perform a timing analysis to ensure that the signals reach their destinations within the specified time limits.

f.   Summary Report :

At the end of the process, a synthesis report is generated, providing information on performance, power consumption and other aspects of the synthesised circuit.

g.   Post-synthesis simulation :

A post-synthesis simulation is often carried out to check the behaviour of the circuit at a lower level after synthesis.

h.   Hardware implementation :

The synthesised Netlist can then be used as input for the placement and routing process, ultimately leading to the manufacture of the integrated circuit.

VHDL synthesis is an essential step in the design flow, transforming design at a high level of abstraction into a concrete representation suitable for hardware implementation on an electronic chip.

6.   Time extraction :

Delay extraction in VHDL refers to the determination of propagation times and delays associated with signals in an electronic circuit described in VHDL. This step is crucial to ensure that the circuit operates in accordance with the timing and performance specifications defined at the design stage.

Some of the key points about delay extraction in VHDL include:

a.   Timing analysis :

Delay extraction involves in-depth analysis of the signal paths through the circuit to identify delays and propagation times.

b.   Delay models :

VHDL design tools, such as synthesizers and simulators, use delay models to estimate the time required to transmit a signal from one point in the circuit to another.

c.   Types of Deadlines :

There are different types of delay, such as logic gate delays, flip-flop switching delays, routing delays, etc. Each type of delay contributes to the total propagation time of a signal through the circuit. Each type of delay contributes to the total propagation time of a signal through the circuit.

d.   Timing constraints :

Designers can specify timing constraints in their VHDL code or in dedicated constraint files to guide the extraction of delays and ensure that the Circuitrespects the timing specifications.

e.   Time Simulation :

Post-synthesis time simulations are often carried out to validate the extracted delays and ensure that the circuit operates correctly in real-life conditions.

f.   Timing reports :

The design tools generate timing reports that provide detailed information on extracted delays, potential violations of timing constraints, and other timing characteristics of the circuit.

g.   Optimising lead times :

Designers can adjust the design to optimise lead times, for example by modifying the logic to reduce critical delays or by reorganising the placement of elements to improve synchronisation.

Extracting delays in VHDL helps to ensure that the circuit meets performance specifications in terms of speed, timing and temporal stability. This enables designers to make informed decisions to optimise the design for specific timing constraints.

7.   Placement and Routing (P&R) :

Placement and routing are two crucial steps in the design of a VHDL architecture that occur after synthesis. These steps aim to determine the physical location of the various circuit elements on the chip (placement) and to establish the connections between these elements (routing).

a.   Placement :

•   Description: Placement involves deciding the physical location of the various circuit elements on the chip. This includes logic gates, flip-flops, memory blocks and other synthesised components.

•   Objective: The main objective of the placement is to optimise the layout of the elements to minimise latency, reduce power consumption and optimise the use of space on the chip.

b.   Routing :

•   Description: Routing consists of establishing physical connections between circuit elements using the resources available on the chip, such as metal tracks and interconnections.

•   Objective: The objective of routing is to ensure correct connectivity while respecting timing constraints and optimising the length of connections to minimise latency.

c.   Placement and Routing Tools :

•   Automated tools : Automated placement and routing tools, integrated with computer-aided design (CAD) software, are used to perform these tasks efficiently and optimally.

•   Constraint Compliance: These tools take account of design constraints, such as timing constraints, routing rules and the physical limitations of the chip.

d.   Post-Placement Analysis and Routing :

Verification: Once placement and routing have been completed, a post placement and routing check is carried out to ensure that the circuit still meets the design specifications and constraints imposed.

e.   Feedback loop :

Optimisation: Depending on the results of the post-placement and routing analysis, adjustments can be made to the design, and a feedback loop with synthesis may be necessary to make further optimisations.

Placement and routing are essential steps in transforming the logic model of the circuit into a physical implementation on a chip. These processes aim to ensure that the circuit respects the design constraints, minimises signal latency and makes efficient use of the chip's resources.

8.   Conclusion

In this section, we have detailed the design flow of embedded architectures based on the VHDL language. In the next chapter, we will describe the fundamental concepts of the language.

CHAPTER 2

Fundamental concepts of the VHDL language

1. Introduction :

The term 'digital systems' encompasses a range of systems from low-level components to complete systems-on-a-chip and board-level designs. If we are to encompass this range of views of digital systems, we need to recognise the complexity we are dealing with. It is not humanly possible to comprehend such complex systems in their entirety. We need to find ways of managing this complexity so that we can, with some degree of confidence, design components and systems that meet their requirements. In this chapter, we will introduce some fundamental concepts of the VHDL language.

2. Embedded system modelling :

The most important way to meet this challenge is to adopt a systematic design methodology. If we start with a requirements document for the system, we can design an abstract structure that meets the requirements. We can then decompose this structure into a set of components that interact to perform the same function. Each of these components can in turn be decomposed until we reach a level where we have ready-made primitive components that perform a required function. The result of this process is a hierarchically composed system, built from the primitive elements.

The advantage of this methodology is that each subsystem can be designed independently of the others. When we use a subsystem, we can think of it as an abstraction rather than having to look at its detailed composition. In this way, at each stage of the design process, we only need to pay attention to the small amount of information that is relevant to the current design objective. In this way, we avoid being overwhelmed by masses of detail.

We use the term model to describe our understanding of a system. The model represents relevant information and abstracts irrelevant details. This implies that there can be several models of the same system, since different information is relevant in different contexts. One type of model may focus on representing the function of the system, while another may represent how the system is made up of sub-systems.

There are a number of important reasons for formalising this idea of a model, including

- express the system requirements in a complete and unambiguous way.
- document the functionality of a system
- test a design to make sure it works properly

3. VHDL modelling concepts :

In this section, we look at the basic VHDL concepts for behavioural and structural modelling. This provides an introduction to VHDL and a foundation for the following chapters. As an example, we look at ways of describing a four-bit register, shown in Figure 2-1.

Using VHDL terminology, we call the reg4 module a design entity, and the inputs and outputs are ports. Figure 3 shows a VHDL description of the interface to this entity. This is an example of an entity declaration. It introduces a name for the entity and lists the input and output ports, specifying that they carry bit values ('0' or '1') into and out of the entity. So we see that an entity declaration describes the external view of the entity.

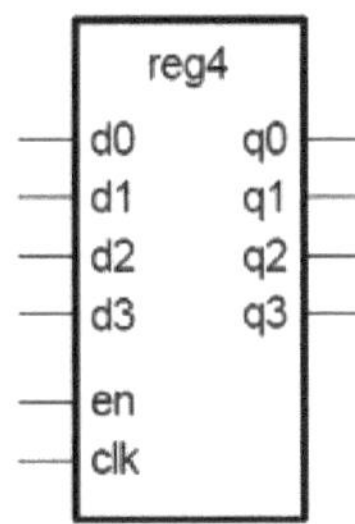

Chapitre 1   3 4-bit register

The 4-bit register is called reg4. This block has 6 inputs and *4* outputs.

The 6 entries can be divided into two parts:

• The specific inputs are: d0, dl, d2 and d3.

These inputs are each 1-bit inputs as described above. As an example, let's assume that the input to our block is an integer with a value between 0 and 15. This value belongs to the interval ['0000','llll']. The :

o   d0represents the   least significant bit   (can be assimilated to the units bit).

o   dlrepresents the   next most significant bit   (the next bit from right to left equals

to the tens bit).

o   d2represents the   next most significant bit   (equivalent to the hundreds bit).

o   d3represents the   most significant bit   (equivalent to the thousands bit).

• The generic entries are: en and clk.

o en or enable: represents the bit corresponding to permission to execute the block set.

o clk or clock: represents the clock cycle used to orchestrate the VHDL code.

The four output signals are q0, ql, q2 and q3. By analogy with the inputs d0, dl, d2 and d3, these outputs represent the result of executing the data input to the block.

The VHDL representation code shown in Figure 4 is as follows:

entity reg4 is

    port (dθ, d1, d2, d3, en, elk : in bit;

                        qθ, q1, q2, q3 : out bit);

end entity reg4;

Figure 4 VHDL code for the register entity

Let's try to analyse the code written :

entity is the term used to demonstrate the start and end of a specific entity. It is a block to be written in VHDL (it is similar to a function in algorithmics).

So the first thing to do is to put **entity** (*entity_name*) followed by **is.**

We then define the inputs, outputs and their types. The term **port** is used to define **d0, d1, d2, d3, en** and **clk** as inputs **(in).** These inputs are of **bit** type. However, **q0, q1, q2** and **q3** are outputs. These outputs are also of **bit** type.

a. Elements of behaviour

In VHDL, the description of the internal implementation of an entity is called the entity architecture body. There can be a number of different architecture bodies for the same entity interface, corresponding to alternative implementations that perform the same function. We can write a behavioural architecture body for an entity, which describes the function in an abstract way. Such a body of architecture includes only process declarations, which are collections of actions to be executed in sequence. These actions are called sequential instructions and are very similar to the types of state we see in a conventional programming language. The types of actions that can be performed include evaluating expressions, assigning values to variables, conditional execution, repeated execution and subroutine calls. In addition, there is a sequential instruction specific to hardware modelling languages, the signal assignment instruction. This instruction is similar to variable assignment, but causes the value of a signal to be updated at a given time.

To illustrate these ideas, let's look at a behavioural architecture body for the reg4 entity, shown in Figure 2-3. In this architecture body, the part following the first **begin** keyword comprises a process declaration, which describes the behaviour of the registry. It begins with the process name, storage, and ends with the keywords **end process.**

The code representing the behavioural results in Figure 3 in VHDL is shown in Figure 5.

The process statement defines a sequence of actions that must take place when the system is simulated. These actions control how the entity's port values change over time, i.e. they control the entity's behaviour. This process can change the values of the entity's ports using signal assignment instructions.

This process works as follows. When the simulation is started, the signal values are set to "0" and the process is activated. The process variables (listed after the **variable** keyword**)** are initialized to "0", then the instructions are executed in order. The first instruction is a *wait instruction* that *suspends* the process. While the process is suspended, it is *sensitive* to the clk signal. When clk takes the value '1', the process resumes.

The next instruction is a condition which tests whether the signal is "1". If so, the instructions between the **then** and **end if** keywords are executed, updating the process variables using the values of the input signals. After the conditional if instruction, four signal assignment instructions are executed, causing the output signals to be updated 5 ns later.

When the process reaches the end of the list of instructions, they are executed again, starting from the **begin** keyword**,** and the cycle is repeated. Note that while the process is suspended, the values of the process variables are not lost. This means that the process can represent the state of a system.

architecture behav of reg4 is begin

storage : **process is**

variable stored. dO, stored. d1, stored. d2, stored. d3 : bit;

begin

wait until clk = 'Γ;

if en = '1' **then**

stored_dO := dθ;

stored_d1 := d1;

stored_d2 := d2;

stored_d3 := d3;

end if;

qθ <= stored_dO **after** 5 ns;

q1 <= stored. d1 after 5 ns;

q2 <= stored_d2 after 5 ns;

q3 <= stored_d3 after 5 ns;

end process storage;

end architecture behav;

Figure 5 Register behaviour code

b. Structural elements :

An architecture body composed solely of interconnected subsystems is called a *structural* architecture body. Figure 6 shows how the reg4 entity can be composed of D-flipflops.

If we want to describe this in VHDL, we will need entity declarations and architecture bodies for the sub-systems, as shown in Figure 7.

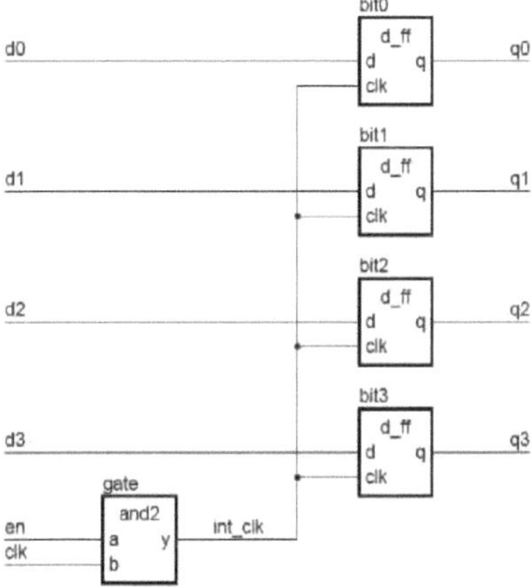

Figure 6 Register behaviour code

```
entity d_ff Is
por( ( d. Clk ; In bit; q : out bit ); end d_ff;
architecture basic of d_ff is
begin

ff. behavlar : process is
begin
wait until elk = T;
q <= d after 2 ns;
end process ff_behaviai;
end architecture basic:
entity ≡ld2 to
port ( a. b ; i⊓ bit y ; cut bit );
and and2;
architecture basic of aⲧd2 la
begin
and2_behavior : process is
begin
y <≡ a and b after 2 ns;
wait on a. b
end process and2_behavtor; end architecture basis;
```

Figure 7 Architecture body in VHDL

Figure 8 is a VHDL architecture body declaration that describes the structure shown in Figure 6. The *signal declaration,* before the **begin** keyword, defines the architecture's internal signals. In this example, the int_clk signal is declared as carrying a C'O' or '1' bit value.) In general, VHDL signals can be declared to carry arbitrarily complex values. In the body of the architecture, entity ports are also treated as signals.

architecture struct **of** reg4 **is**

int **signal**. clk : bit;

begin

bitθ **: entity** work.d_ff(basic)

11

port map (dθ, int_clk, qO);

bit 1: **entity** work.d_ff(basic)

port map (d1, int_clk, q1);

bit2 : **entity** work.d_ff(basic)

port map (d2, int_clk, q2);

bit3: **entity** work.d_ff(basic)

port map (d3, int_clk, q3);

gate : **entity** work.and2(basic)

port map (en, elk, int. clk);

end architecture struct;

Figure 8 Body of the structural architecture of the reg4 entity

In the second part of the architecture body, a number of *component instances* are created, representing the sub-systems from which the reg4 entity is composed. Each component instance is a copy of the entity representing the sub-system, using the corresponding base architecture body. (The name work refers to the current working library, in which all entity and architecture body descriptions are assumed to be kept).

The *port map[8]* specifies the connection of the ports of each component instance to the signals of the body of the architecture that surrounds it. For example, bitO, an instance of the d_ff entity, has its d port connected to the dθ signal, its clk port connected to the int_clk signal and its q port connected to the qO signal.

c. The testbench :

We often test a VHDL model using an enveloping model called a *testbench*. This name comes from the analogy with a real hardware test bench, on which a device under test is stimulated by signal generators and observed by signal probes. A VHDL test bench consists of an architecture body containing an instance of the component to be tested and processes that generate sequences of values on signals connected to the component instance. The architecture body can also contain processes that test that the component instance produces the expected values on its output signals. Alternatively, we can use the monitoring functions of a simulator to observe the outputs.

A testbed model for the behavioural implementation of the reg4 register is shown in Figure 9. The entity declaration does not include a list of ports, since the testbed is entirely self-contained. The body of the architecture contains signals connected to the input and output ports of the component instance dut, the device under test. The process called stimulus provides a sequence of test values on the input signals by executing signal assignment instructions, interspersed with wait instructions. We can use a simulator to observe the values of signals qO to q3 to check that the register is operating correctly. When all the stimulus values have been applied, the stimulus process waits indefinitely, ending the simulation.

The addition of **wait for** expressions allows you to wait 20 ns before moving on to the next instruction. The same applies to the **after** expression.

It is important to note that VHDL code is parallel in architecture. To execute sequential code, a **process** must be inserted.

entity test. bench **is end entity** test. bench;

architecture test_reg4 **of** test_bench **is**

signal dθ, d1, d2, d3, en, elk, qθ, q1, q2, q3: bit;

Ibegin

dut : entity work.reg4(behav)

port map (dθ, d1, d2, d3, en, elk, qθ, q1, q2, q3);

stimulus : **process is begin**

dθ<='1'; d1 <= 1ᵤ ; d2<='1'; d3<='1ʹ ;

en <= 0'; elk <= '0ʹ ;

wait for 10 ns;

en <= 'Г; **wait for** 10 ns;

elk = '1', '0' **after** 10 ns; **wait for** 20 ns;

dθ <= 0'; d1 <= '0'; d2 <= '0'; d3 <= '0';

en <= 0'; **wait for** 10 ns;

elk <= '1', '0' **after** 10 ns; **wait for** 20 ns;

wait;

end process stimulus;

end architecture test_reg4;   "

Figure 9 Testbench model for 1 test_reg4 architecture

4. Conclusion :

In this chapter, we have described the fundamentals of the VHDL language. We started with the structure of the entity, followed by the architecture that allows behavioural data to be viewed. Finally, we close with the Testbench. The Testbench uses the reg4 entity to test its execution. The results of Testbench execution are obtained using software such as Isim or Modeslim. In the next chapter, we will define the VHDL construction or, more specifically, how to use VHDL as a programming language.

CHAPTER 3

VHDL construction

1. Introduction :

Having previously described the various basic elements that make it possible to code in VHDL, such as entities, architectures and the testbench, in this chapter we will explain how a system can be built in VHDL. We will propose the various syntactic elements that enable VHDL to be used as a programming language.

2. List of variables :

When we learn a new language, we have to learn how to write the basics, such as numbers and identifiers. We also need to learn syntax, the rules of grammar that govern how we form linguistic constructions. We'll briefly describe the lexical elements and our notation of the grammar rules, and then we'll start to introduce the features of the language.

VHDL uses the ISO 8859 Latin-I 8-bit character set. This set includes upper and lower case letters (including letters with diacritical marks, such as 'to', 'at', etc.), digits from0to9, punctuation and other special characters.

a. Comments

When we write a hardware model in VHDL, it is important to annotate the code with comments. A VHDL model consists of a number of lines of text. A comment can be added to a line by writing two dashes together, followed by the text of the comment. For example :

-- one line of VHDL description   -- a descriptive comment

The comment extends from the two dashes to the end of the line and can include any text, since it is not formally part of the VHDL model. The code of a model can include empty lines and lines containing only comments, beginning with two dashes. We can write long comments on successive lines, each beginning with two dashes, for example :

-    - The following code models
-    - the system control section
... some VHDL code ...

It is important to note certain criteria of the VHDL language. The following naming conventions apply to VHDL designs:

-    VHDL is not case-sensitive.
-    Two dashes are used to start comment lines.
-    Names can use alphanumeric characters and the underscore " ".
-    Names must begin with an alphabetical letter.
-    It is forbidden to use two underscores in succession or to use an underscore as the last character of the name.
-    Spaces are not allowed in names.
-    Object names must be unique. For example, you cannot have a signal named A and a bus named A(7 to 0).

Here is a list of reserved VHDL keywords [9] :

Abs	Downto	Library	postponed	Subtype
Access	Else	Linkage	procedure	Then
After	Elsif	Literal	process	To
Alias	End	Loop	pure	Transport
All	Entity	Map	range	Type
And	Exit	Mod	record	Unaffected
Architecture	File	Nand	register	Units
Array	For	New	reject	Until
Assert	Function	Next	rem	Use

Attribute	Generate	Nor	report	Variable
Begin	Generic	Not	return	Wait
Block	Group	Null	Rol	When
Body	Guarded	of	Ror	While
Buffer	If	We	select	With
Bus	Impure	Open	severity	Xnor
Case	In	Gold	shared	Xor
Component	Inertial	Others	signal	Configuration
Inout	Out	Sla	constant	Is
Package	Sra	disconnect	label	Port
Srl				

b.   Figures

Two forms of numbers can be written in VHDL code: integers and real numbers. An integer literal simply represents a whole number and consists of digits without a decimal point. Real literals, on the other hand, can represent fractional numbers. They always include a decimal point, which is preceded by at least one digit and followed by at least one digit. Here are some examples of decimal integers

23 0 146

Here are some examples of real literals

23.10.0 3.14159

Integers and reals can also use exponential notation, in which the number is followed by the letter "E" or "e" and an exponent value. The exponent indicates a power of 10 by which the number is multiplied. For integers, the exponent must not be negative, whereas for real numbers, it can be positive or negative. Here are some examples of integer literals using exponential notation

46E5 1E+12 19e00

Here are some examples of real literals using exponential notation

1.234E09 98.6E+21 34.0e-08

c.   Characters :

A literal character can be written in VHDL code by enclosing it in single quotes. Any printable character in the standard character set (including a space character) can be written in this way. Here are a few examples

'A'   --upper-case letter

'z'   --lower-case letter

','   --the   punctuation character comma

-- the single inverted comma punctuation character

-- the space separator character

d.   Strings :

A character string represents a sequence of characters and is written by enclosing the characters in inverted commas. The string can contain any number of characters (including zero), but it must fit entirely on one line. Here are a few examples

"A string

"We can include any printing characters (e.g., &%@⌐*) in a string!!!"

"00001111ZZZZ" "" - empty string

If we need to include a character in quotes in a string, we write two characters in quotes together. The pair is interpreted as a single character in the string. For example:

"A string within a string: "A chain". "

If we need to write a character string that doesn't fit on one line, we can use the concatenation operator ("&") to join two substrings. For example, the concatenation operator

"If a chain doesn't fit on a line, "

then we can divide it into parts on separate lines".

e.   Bit Stirngs

The VHDL language includes values that represent bits (binary digits), which can be either "0" or "1". A bit string literal represents a sequence of these binary values. It is represented by a string of digits, surrounded by double quotes and preceded by a character that specifies the base of the digits. The base specifier can be one of the following:

- B for binary,
- for octal (base 8) and
- X for hexadecimal (base 16).

For example, some literal bit strings specified in binary are as follows

B "0100011" B "10" b "1111_0010_0001" B " "

Note that we can include underscore characters in bit string literals to make the literal more readable. The base specifier can be upper or lower case. The last of the above examples shows an empty bit string.

If the base specifier is octal, the digits "0" to "7" can be used. Each digit represents exactly three bits in the sequence. Here are a few examples

0 "372" -- equivalent to B "011_lll_010"

o "00" -- equivalent toB "000_000"

If the base specifier is hexadecimal, the digits "0" to "9" and "A" to "F" or "a" to "f" (representing 10 to 15) can be used. In hexadecimal, each digit represents exactly four bits. Here are a few examples

X "FA" -- equivalent toB "llll_1010

X "0d" -- equivalent to B "0000_1101".

3.   List of variables :

In this tutorial, we describe syntax rules using a notation based on the Backus-Naur extended form (EBNF). The idea behind EBNF is to divide the language into syntactic categories. For each syntactic category, we write a rule that describes how to construct a VHDL clause of that category by combining lexical elements and clauses from other categories. We write a rule with the syntactic category we define on the line to the left of a sign (read "is defined as"), and a pattern to the right. The simplest type of pattern is a collection of elements in sequence, for example :

variable_assignment target := expression ;

This rule indicates that a VHDL clause of the "variable_assignment" category is defined as a clause of the "target" category, followed by the symbol followed by a clause of the "expression" category, followed by the " symbol.

The next type of rule to consider is one that allows an optional component in a clause. We indicate the optional part by placing it between the symbols "[" and "]". For example

function_call name [(associationjist)]

This indicates that a function call consists of a name that can be followed by a list of associations in brackets. Note the use of contour symbols to write the pattern in the ruler, as opposed to normal solid symbols which are VHDL lexical elements.

In many rules, it is necessary to specify that a clause is optional, but that if it is present, it can be repeated as many times as necessary. For example, in this rule

process_statement

process is

{ process_declarative_item } **begin**

{ Sequential-Statement} **end process**

The braces specify that a process may include zero or more declarative process elements and zero or more sequential instructions. A common case in VHDL rules is a model consisting of a category followed by zero or more repeats of that category. In this case, we use dots inside the braces to represent the repeated category, rather than writing it out again in full. Here's an example of the rule:

case_statement **case** expression **is** case_statement_alternative **{ ... } end case ;**

It specifies that a list of identifiers is made up of one or more identifiers and that, if there is more than one, they are separated by commas. Note that dots always represent a repetition of the category immediately preceding the left brace symbol. So, in the rule above, it is the identifier that is repeated, not the comma. Many syntax rules allow a category to be composed of a certain number of alterations, specified using the 'I' symbol. For example, the rule specifies that the category 'mode' can be formed from a clause composed of 1 'one of the reserved words chosen from the alternatives listed.

mode **in I out I inout**

The final notation we use in our syntax rules is parenthetical grouping, using the symbols and These symbols are simply used to group a part of a pattern, in order to avoid any ambiguity that might arise. For example, the inclusion of parenthetical theses in the rule makes it clear that a factor can be followed by one of the operator symbols, and then by another factor

term factor { (* I / I mod I rem) factor }

This EBNF notation is sufficient to describe the complete VHDL grammar. However, a VHDL description is often subject to other constraints relating to the meaning of the constructs used. To express these constraints, many rules include additional information about the meaning of a language feature. For example, the rule above describing how a function call is formed is completed in the following way:

function_call function_name [(parameter_association_list) **]**

The italicised prefix on a syntax category in the model simply provides semantic information. This rule indicates that the name cannot be just any name, but must be the name of a function. Similarly, the list of associations must describe the parameters supplied to the function.

In this tutorial, we will introduce each new VHDL feature by describing its syntax using EBNF rules, and then describe the meaning and use of the feature using examples. In many cases, we will start with a simplified version of the syntax to make it easier to learn the description and we will return to the full details in a later section.

4. Constants and variables :

Constants and variables are objects in which data can be stored for use in a model. The difference between the two is that the value of a constant cannot be modified once it has been created, whereas the value of a variable can be modified as many times as required using variable assignment instructions.

Constants and variables must be declared before they can be used in a model. A declaration simply introduces the name of the object, defines its type and can give it an initial value. The syntax rule for declaring a constant is as follows

constant_declaration

constant identifier **{ ,... }** : SubtypeJndication := expression ;

Here are some examples of constant declarations:

constant number_of_bytes : integer := 4;

constant number_of_bits : integer :=8* number_of_bytes;

constant e : real := 2.718281828;

constant prop_delay : time := 3 ns;

constant Size_limit, Count_limit : integer := 255;

The form of a variable declaration is similar to that of a constant declaration. The syntax rule is as follows:

declaration_variable

variable identifier { ,... } : Subtype_indication [:= expression] ;

The initialization expression is optional; if we omit it, the default initial value assigned to the variable when it is created depends on the type. For scalar types, the default initial value is the leftmost value of the type. For example, for integers, this is the smallest representable integer. Here are some examples of variable declarations

variable index : integer := 0;

variable sum, average, largest : real;

variable start, finish : time :=0ns;

Declarations of constants and variables can appear in several places in a VHDL model, including in the process declaration parts. In this case, the declared object can only be used within the process. One of the restrictions on the location of a variable declaration is that it cannot be placed in such a way that the variable is accessible to more than one process. This avoids the strange effects that could occur if processes modified the variable in an indeterminate order. Once a variable has been declared, its value can be modified by an assignment instruction. The syntax of a variable assignment instruction is given by the following rule

variable_assignment_statement name := expression ;

The name in a variable assignment statement identifies the variable to be modified, and the expression is evaluated to produce the new value. The type of this value must match the type of the variable. Here are some examples of assignment statements:

program_counter := 0;

index := index + 1;

The first assignment sets the value of the program_counter variable to zero, replacing any previous value. The second example increments the index value by one.

5.   Conclusion

In this chapter we have defined some constants and variables that are used in VHDL. In the next chapter, we will present some VHDL exercises.

CHAPTER 4

Basic constructions and functionalities in VHDL

1.   Introduction :

After describing the subtleties of the VHDL language, we moved on to the construction of VHDL by presenting the processes, architectures, etc. In this chapter, we will describe the entity, architectures and various functions used in the VHDL language. In this chapter, we will describe the entity, architectures and various functions used in the VHDL language.

2.   Declaration of an entity :

First, let's look at the syntax rules for an entity declaration and then show some examples. The syntax rules are as follows:

entity_declaration <=
entity identifier **is**
[**port** { /?ort_interfacejist) ;]
end [**entity** [identify] :
InterfaceJist <=
i identify {,...JJ mode] SubtypeJndication
mode <= **in I out I inout**

The identifier in an entity declaration names the module so that it can be referred to later. If the identifier is included at the end of the declaration, it must repeat the name of the entity.

The port clause names each of the ports which, together, form the entity's interface. We can think of ports as analogous to pins in a circuit; they are the means by which information is introduced into and extracted from the circuit.

In VHDL, each port of an entity has a type, which specifies the type of information that can be communicated, and a mode, which specifies whether the information enters or leaves the entity through the port. Here is a simple example of an entity declaration

entity adder **is**

port {a,b: **in** bit;

sum : **out** stdJogic_vector{ldowntoO));

end entity adder;

This example describes an entity called an adder, with two bit input ports and a two-bit vector output port (from the most significant bit to the least significant (stdJogic_vector{ldowntoOJ). We can list the ports in any order; we don't have to put inputs before outputs.

In this example, we have input and output ports. We can also have bidirectional ports, with **inout** mode, to model devices that alternately sense and drive data through a pin. These models need to take into account the possibility that more than one connected device is driving a given signal at the same time. VHDL provides a mechanism for this, called *signal resolution.*

Note that the port clause is optional. We can therefore write an entity declaration which describes a completely autonomous module. As the name of this example suggests, this type of module generally represents the top level of a design hierarchy.

entity topjevel **is end entity** topjevel;

We have described the entity that represents the header of our VHDL function. This entity includes the inputs and outputs of each code written. In this section, we will present the architecture. The architecture represents the intrinsic operation of each block implemented.

3.   Architectural bodies :

The internal operation of a module is described by an architecture body. An architecture body generally applies certain operations to the values of the input ports, generating values to be assigned to the output ports.

Operations can be described either by processes, which contain sequential instructions operating on values, or by a collection of components representing sub-circuits. When the operation requires the generation of intermediate values, these can be described using signals, analogous to the internal threads of a module. The syntax rule for architecture bodies is described by the following code:

architecture_body <=∎

architecture identifier **of** ew/7(y_name **is**

{ block_declarative_item }

begin

{ Competitor-Statement }

end [**architecture**] [identify] ;

The identifier names this particular architecture body and the entity name specifies the module whose operation is described by this architecture body. If the identifier is included at the end of the architecture body, it must repeat the name of the architecture body.

There may be several different architecture bodies corresponding to a single entity, each describing a different way of implementing the module's operation. The declarative block elements of an architecture body are the declarations needed to implement the operations. These elements can include type and constant declarations, signal declarations and other types of declarations that we will look at in later chapters.

The concurrent declarations of an architecture body describe the operation of the module. One form of concurrent declaration, which we have already seen, is the process declaration. We started by looking at processes because they are the most basic form of concurrent declaration. All other forms can be reduced to one or more processes. Concurrent instructions are so called because, conceptually, they can be activated and perform their actions together, i.e. simultaneously. Conversely, sequential instructions within a process are executed one after the other. Concurrency is useful for modelling the behaviour of real circuits.

When we need to provide internal signals in the body of an architecture, we need to define them using signal declarations. The syntax of a signal declaration is very similar to that of a variable declaration:

This declaration simply names each signal, specifies its type and includes

SignaLdeclaration <=

signal identifier   subtype_indication [:= expression] ;

possibly an initial value for all the signals declared in the declaration.

An important point we mentioned earlier is that the entity's ports are also visible to processes inside the body of the architecture and are used in the same way as signals. This corresponds to our view of ports as external pins on a circuit: from the internal point of view, a pin is just a wire with an external connection. It therefore makes sense for VHDL to treat ports as signals within an entity architecture.

4.   Behavioural description:

At the most basic level, the behaviour of a module is described by signal assignment instructions within processes. We can think of a process as the basic unit of behaviour description. A process is executed in response to changes in signal values and uses the current values of the signals it receives to determine new values for other signals.

The assignment of a signal is a sequential statement and can therefore only occur within a process. In this section, we look in detail at the interaction between signals and processes.

a.   Signal assignment

In all the examples we've looked at so far, we've used a simple form of signal assignment declaration. Each assignment simply provides a new value for a signal. What we haven't addressed yet is the question of timing: when does the signal take on its new value? This question is fundamental to hardware modelling, in which events occur over time. Let's look first at the syntax of a basic signal assignment instruction in a process:

signal_assignment_statement <=

name <. (^expressl0n | >fter ^expression]) (.) ;

The syntax rule tells us that we can specify one or more expressions, each with an optional delay. It is these delays in a signal assignment that allow us to specify when the new value should be applied. Let's take the following assignment as an example:

y <= **not** or_a_b **after** 5 ns;

This specifies that the y signal must take on the new value at a time 5 ns later than when the instruction is executed. So, if the above assignment is executed at time 250 ns and or_a_b has the value "1" at that time, the y signal will take the value "0" at time 255 ns. Note that the instruction itself is executed in a time considered to be zero.

The time dimension referred to when the model is run is the simulation time, i.e. the time during which the modelled circuit is expected to operate. We measure simulation time by starting from zero at the beginning of execution and increasing in discrete steps as events occur in the model. A simulator must have a simulation time clock and, when a signal assignment instruction is executed, the specified delay is added to the current simulation time to determine when the new value should be applied to the signal. We say that the signal assignment schedules a transaction for the signal, where the transaction consists of the new value and the simulation time at which it is to be applied. When the simulation time advances to the time when a transaction is scheduled, the signal is updated with the new value. We say that the signal is *active* during this simulation cycle. If the new value is not equal to the old value that it replaces on a signal, we say that an *event* occurs on the signal. The importance of this distinction lies in the fact that processes react to events on signals, not transactions.

The syntax rules for signal assignments show that we can program a number of transactions for a signal, to be applied after different delays. For example, a clock driver process might execute the following assignment to generate the next two edges of a clock signal (assuming T_pw is a constant representing the pulse width of the clock)

Λ<=·1· after T_pw, 0' after 2*T_pw;

If this instruction is executed at simulation time 50 ns and T_pw has a value of 10 ns, a transaction is scheduled at time 60 ns to set clk to '1', and a second transaction is scheduled at time 70 ns to set clk to '0'. If we assume that clk has the value '0' when the assignment is executed, both transactions produce events on clk.

Let's try to set up a process that models a two-input multiplexer. The value of the sel port is used to select the signal assignment to be executed to determine the output value.

mux : process (a, b, sel) is

begin

case sel is

when '0' =>

z <= a after prop_delay;

when '1' =>

z <= b after prop_delay;

end case;

end process mux;

A process is said to define a driver for a signal if and only if it contains at least one signal assignment instruction for that signal. If a process contains signal assignment instructions for several signals, it defines drivers for each of these signals. A driver is a source for a signal in that it provides values to be applied to the signal. An important rule to remember is that for normal signals, there can only be one source. This means that we cannot write two different processes each containing signal assignment states for the same signal. If we want to model things like buses or wired signals, we have to use a special type of signal called a resolved signal, which we'll talk about later.

b.   Signal attributes :

VHDL provides a number of attributes for signals to find information about their transaction and event history. Given a signal S and a value T of type time, VHDL defines the following attributes:

S'delayed(T)   A signal which takes the same values as S but is delayed by a time T

S'eventTrue   if there is an event on S in the current simulation cycle, false otherwise   .

S'last_event Interval of time elapsed since the last event on S S'last_value Value of S just before the last event on S.

These attributes are often used to check the temporal behaviour of a model. For example, we can check that a signal with a minimum configuration time of Tsu before a rising edge on a clk clock of type std_ulogic as follows:

if clk'event and (clk = '1' or clk = 'H')

and (clk'last. value = 'O' or clk'last. value = 'L') than

assert d'last_event >= Tsu

report "Timing error: d changed within setup time of clk"; end if;

Consider the following VHDL code. Let's try to understand what it is used for.

entity edge_triggered_Dff is

port (D : in bit; clk : in bit; clr : in bit;

Q : out bit);

end entity edge_triggered_Dff;

architecture behavioral of edge_triggered_Dff is

begin

state_change : process (clk, clr) is begin

if clr = 'I' then

Q <= 'O' after 2 ns;

elsif clk'event and clk = 'I' then

Q <= D after 2 ns;

end if;

end process state change;

end architecture behavioral;

We can test the rising edge of a clock signal to model an edge-triggered flip-flop. The latch loads the value of its input D on a rising edge of clk, but clears the outputs asynchronously whenever clr is '1'. The entity declaration and a body of behavioural architecture are illustrated by the preceding code, which follows.

c.   The wait instruction :

Now that we've seen how to change signal values over time, the next step in behavioural modelling is to specify when processes react to changes in signal values. To do this, we use wait instructions. A wait statement is a sequential statement with the following syntax rule Wait-Statement <=

wait | on *signal~name*

until *boolea".*expression **for** ", "expression] ;

The purpose of the wait instruction is to cause the process executing the report to suspend execution. The *sensitivity* clause, the *condition* clause and the *delay* clause specify when the process should resume execution. We can include any combination of these clauses or omit all three. Let's go through each clause and describe what it specifies.

The sensitivity clause, which begins with the word **on,** allows us to specify a list of signals to which the process responds. If we simply include a sensitivity clause in a wait statement, the process will resume whenever one of the listed signals changes value, i.e. whenever an event occurs on one of the signals. This type of wait statement is useful in a process that models a combinatorial logic block, since any change to the inputs can result in new output values; for example: **half. add : process is**

Ibegin

sum <= a xor b after T_pd;

carry <= a and b after T_pd;

wait on a, b;

end process half.add:

This form of process is so common in digital system modelling that VHDL provides the abbreviated notation we have seen in many examples in previous chapters. A process with a sensitivity list in its header is exactly equivalent to a process with a wait instruction at the end, containing a sensitivity clause naming the signals in the sensitivity list. Thus, the half_add process above could be rewritten as shown in the following code:

half_add : process (a, b) is

Ibegin

sum <= a xor b after T_pd;

carry <= a and b after T_pd;

end process half.add;

The conditional clause of a wait instruction, which begins with the word **until, is** used to specify a condition that must be true for the process to resume. For example, the wait instruction causes the running process to be suspended until the value of the clk signal changes to "1". **wait until** clk = 'T;

The condition expression is tested while the process is suspended to determine whether it should be resumed. If the **wait** instruction does not contain a sensitivity clause, the condition is tested each time an event occurs on one of the signals mentioned in the condition.

wait on Clkuntilreset = O':

If a wait instruction includes a sensitivity clause as well as a condition clause, the condition is only tested when an event occurs on one of the signals in the sensitivity clause. For example, if a process is suspended on the next wait instruction. The condition is tested each time the value of clk changes, independently of any change on reset.

The timeout clause in a wait statement, starting with the word for, allows you to specify a maximum simulation time interval during which the process should be suspended. If we also include a sensitivity or condition clause, these clauses can cause the process to resume earlier. For example, the wait statement causes the running process to be suspended until the trigger takes the value "1" or until 1ms of simulation time has elapsed, whichever occurs first. If we simply include a timeout clause in a wait statement, the process will be suspended for the specified time.

wait until trigger = '1' for 1 ms;

d.   Declaration of a process :

We have used processes extensively in the examples in this and previous chapters, so we have seen most of the details of writing and using them. To summarise, let's now look at the formal syntax of a process declaration and a process revision operation. The content of a process is characterised by the use of sequential instructions. In fact, just as in an architecture in which instructions are executed in parallel, in a process instructions are executed sequentially. The syntax rule used in an estia process is as follows: process_statement <=

process_label : **process [(** *signal_name* **{,..})][is**
{ process_declarative_item }
begin
{ Sequential-Statement }
end process [pro ∞s Jabd] :
The declarative elements of a process instruction can include declarations of constants, types and variables, as well as other declarations that we will discuss later. The sequential instructions that form the body of the process can include all those we introduced earlier, as well as signal assignment and wait instructions. When a process is activated during simulation, it starts executing from the first sequential instruction and continues until it reaches the last. It then starts again from the first. This would be an infinite loop, with no progress in the simulation, if there were no wait instructions, which suspend execution of the process until an important event occurs. Wait instructions are the only instructions whose execution requires a simulation time greater than zero. It is only by executing the wait instructions that the simulation time increases.

A process can include a sensitivity list in brackets after the **process** keyword. The sensitivity list identifies a set of signals that the process monitors for events. If the sensitivity list is omitted, the process must include one or more wait instructions. On the other hand, if the sensitivity list is included, the process body cannot contain any wait instructions. Instead, there is an implicit wait statement, just before the **end process** keywords, which includes the signals listed in the sensitivity list as signals in an **on** clause.

e.   Declarations of assignment of conditional signals

The conditional signal assignment statement is a concurrent statement that provides a short hand for a process containing a collection of ordinary signal assignments in an if statement. The syntax rule is as follows:

conditional_signal_assignment <=

name <= { waveform **when** *boolean-expression* **else** } waveform | **when** ⅛₀₀ ⅛^exprcs s∞n | ;

Conditional signal assignment allows us to specify which of a number of waveforms should be assigned to a signal depending on the values of certain conditions. For example, the following statement is a functional description of a multiplexer, with four data inputs (dO, dl, d2 and d3), two select inputs (selO and sell) and one data output (z). All these signals are bit signals.

z <=d0 **when** sell   = '0'   **and**   sel0 = '0'   **else**
d1 **when** sell = '0'   **and**   sel0 = '1'   **else**
d2 **when** sell =·1'   **and**   sel0 = '0'   **else**
d3 **when** sell = T   **and**   sel0 = ·1· ;

f.   Assignment declarations for selected signals

The selected signal assignment instruction is similar in many ways to the conditional signal assignment instruction. It is shorthand for a process containing a number of ordinary signal assignments within a case instruction. The syntax rule is selected_signal_assignment <≠ **with** expression **select**

name <= { waveform **when** choices , ; waveform **when** choices ;

This instruction allows us to choose from a number of waveforms to associate with a signal, depending on the value of an expression. Here's an example:

with alu_function select

with alu_function **select**
    result <=   a + b **after** Tpd   **when** alu_add | alu_add_unsigned,
                   a − b **after** Tpd   **when** alu_sub | alu_sub_unsigned,
                   a **and** b **after** Tpd   **when** alu_and,
                   a **or** b **after** Tpd   **when** alu_or,
                   a **after** Tpd   **when** alu_pass_a;

A selected signal assignment instruction is sensitive to all the signals in the selector expression and the expressions to the right of the assignment arrow. This means that the selected signal assignment above is sensitive to alu_function, a and b.

5.   Structural description:

The structural description of a system is expressed in terms of subsystems interconnected by signals. Each subsystem can in turn be composed of an interconnection of subsystems, and so on, until we finally reach a level composed of primitive elements, described only in terms of behaviour. In this way, the top-level system can be seen as having a hierarchical structure. In this section, we will see how to write structural architecture bodies to express this hierarchical organisation.

We saw earlier in this chapter that concurrent declarations of an architecture body describe an implementation of an entity interface. To write a structural implementation, we need to use a concurrent statement called a *component instantiation* statement, the simplest form of which is governed by the following syntax rule.

component_instantiation_statenient <=

instantiationti-abti

entity ez/iîfy_name (architec⅛zzʲ -identifier) **port map** (port_association_list) ;

This form of component instantiation declaration performs direct Tinstanciation of an entity. We can think of Tinstanciation of components as the creation of a copy of the named entity, with the body of the corresponding architecture substituted for the component instance.

The port map specifies which ports of the entity are connected to which signals in the body of the architecture surrounding it. The simplified syntax rule for a port association list is as follows

'port_association_list <=

([port-name => | ⅛ₖ ⅛name){....}

Each element of the association list associates a port of the entity with a signal of the surrounding architecture body. Let's take a few examples to illustrate component instantiation declarations and the association of ports with signals. Suppose we have an entity declared as the following DRAM controller: entity DRAM-Controller is

port (rd, wr, mem : in bit;

ras, cas, we, ready : out bit);

end entity DRAM-Controller;

A corresponding architecture called fpld. We could create an instance of this entity as follows:

main_mem_controller : entity work.DRAM_controller(fpld)

port map (cpu_rd, cpu_wr, cpu_mem,

mem_ras, mem_cas mem_we, cpu_rdy);

In this example, the name work refers to the current working library in which the entities and architecture bodies are stored. We'll come back to libraries in the next section. The port map in this example lists the signals in the surrounding architecture body to which the ports in the copy of the entity are connected. Positional association is used: each signal listed in the port map is connected to the port located at the same position in the entity declaration. Thus, the cpu_rd signal is connected to the rd port, the cpu_wr signal is connected to the wr port, and so on.

6.   Conclusion:

In this chapter, we have described how entities and architectures are declared. We then presented the behavioural description and all its subtleties. Finally, we conclude with the structural description.

26

CHAPTER 5

Corrected VHDL exercises

1. Introduction :

After describing the subtleties of the VHDL language, we moved on to VHDL construction, presenting processes, architectures, etc. In this chapter, we will present a series of corrected VHDL exercises. In this chapter, we propose a series of corrected VHDL exercises.

2. Flip-flop register [10]:

a. Scales [registers]

Flip-flops, also known as registers, are inferred in VHDL using wait and if statements within a process using a rising edge or falling edge detection, rising edge or falling edge detection expression. Two types of expression can be used: an "event attribute" or a "function call" function call. For example :

[clk'event and clk='l'] -rising edge event attribute

[clk'event et clk='0'] -falling edge 'event attribute rising_edge[clock] -rising edge function call falling_edge[clock] -falling edge function call

The examples in this guide use rising edge event attribute expressions, but falling edge expressions could be used. The event attribute expression is used because some VHDL synthesis tools do not recognise function call expressions.

However, using a function call expression is preferable for simulation, as a function call only detects an edge transition [0to Ioul to 1].

[0 to 1 or 1 to 0] but not a transition from X to 1 or from 0 to X, which may not be a valid transition. This is particularly true when using a multi-valued data type such as StdJogic, which has nine possible values [U, X, 0,1, Z, W, L, H, -].

This section describes and gives examples of different types of flip-flop. See "Registers" on page 63 for information on using specific registers.

b. Rising edge rocker

The following examples show a D flip-flop without asynchronous or synchronous reset or preset. This flip-flop is a sequential cell. Figure 10 shows the rising edge flip-flop.

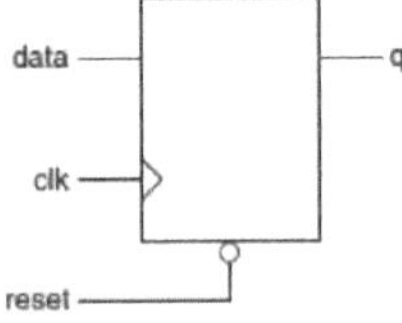

Figure 10 Rocker with rising edge

The VHDL code that represents it is the following: **library** IEEE;

use IEEE.std_logic_1164.all;

entity dff_async_rst **is**

port (data, elk, reset : **in** StdJogic;

q : **out** StdJogic);

end dff_async_rst;

architecture behav **of** dff_async_rst **is**

begin

process (elk, reset) **begin**

if (reset = '0') **then**

q <= '0';

elsif (clk'eventand elk = '1') **then**

q <= data;

end if;

end process;

end behav;

c.   Rising edge flip-flop with asynchronous reset and presetting

Let's try to modify our flip-flop by adding a reset on the one hand and an asynchronous preset on the other. Figure 11 shows this improved flip-flop.

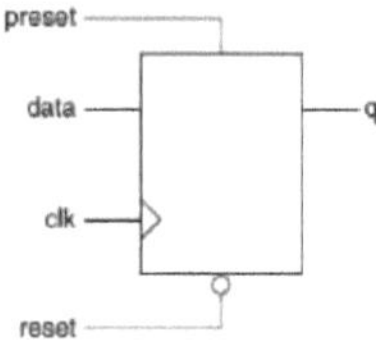

Figure 11 Rising edge flip-flop with asynchronous reset and preset

The VHDL code that represents it is as follows:

IEEE **library**;

use IEEE.std_logic_1164.all;

entity dff_async **is**

port (data, elk, reset, preset : **in** StdJogic;

q : **out** StdJogic);

end dff_async;

architecture behav **of** dff_async **is**

begin

process (elk, reset, preset) **begin**

if (reset = '0') **then**

q <= '0';

elsif (preset = '1') **then**

∇ : ? !

elsif (elk event **and** elk = 1) **then**

q <= data;

end if;

end process;

end behav;

3. Priority encoders using the If-Then-Else instruction

An if-then-else statement is used to conditionally execute sequential statements based on a value. Each condition in the instruction is checked in order against that value until a true condition is found. The associated instructions are then executed and the rest of the instruction is ignored. The if-then-else instructions must be used to give priority to a signal that arrives late. In the following examples, illustrated in Figure 12.

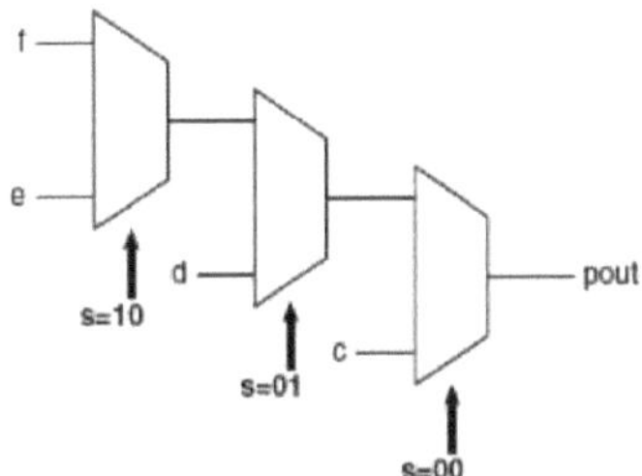

Figure 12 Priority encoder

The VHDL code that represents it is as follows:

```vhdl
IEEE library;
use IEEE.std_logic_1164.all;
entity my_if is
port (c, d, e, f: in StdJogic;
s : in std_logic_vector(l downto 0j;
pout : out StdJogic];
end my_if;
architecture my_arc of my_if is
begin
myif_pro: process (s, c, d, e, f] begin
if s = "OO "then
pout <= c;
elsif s = "01" then
pout <= d;
elsif s = "10" then
pout <= e;
else pout <= f;
end if;
end process myif_pro;
end my_arc;
```

4. Multiplexers :

A case instruction involves parallel coding. Use a case statement to select one of a sequence of alternative statements based on the value of a condition, based on the value of a condition. The condition is checked against each choice in the case instruction until a match is found. The instructions associated with the corresponding choice are then 35 executed. The case statement must include all possible values for a condition or include a default choice to be executed if none of the choices match. The following examples infer multiplexers using a case statement.

VHDL synthesis tools automatically assume parallel operation with no priority in case instructions.

Figure 13 shows a multiplexer.

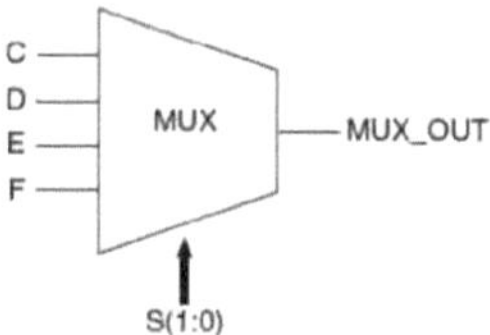

Figure 13 Priority encoder

The VHDL code that represents it is as follows:

```
--4:1 Multiplexor
IEEE library;
use IEEE.std_logic_1164.all;
entity mux is
port (C, D,E,F: in StdJogic;
S :in std_logic_vector(l downto O);
mux_out : out StdJogic);
end mux;
architecture my_mux of mux is
begin
muxl: process (S, C, D, E, F) begin
case s is
when "00" => muxout <= C;
when "01" => muxout <= D;
when "10" => muxout <= E;
when others => muxout <= F;
end case;
end process muxl;
end my_mux;
```

5. Counters :

Counters Count the number of occurrences of an event, either randomly or at uniform intervals. You can infer a counter in your design. However, most synthesis tools cannot infer optimal implementations of counters greater than 8-bits.

a. 8-bit up counter with count enable and asynchronous reset The following example derives an 8-bit up counter with count enable and asynchronous reset.

```
IEEE library;
use IEEE.std_logic_1164.all;
use IEEE.std_logic_unsigned.all;
use IEEE.std_logic_arith.all;
entity counter8 is
port (elk, en, rst : in StdJogic;
```

```vhdl
count : out std_logic_vector (7 downto 0));
end counter8;
architecture behav of counters is
signal ent: std_logic_vector (7 downto 0);
begin
process (elk, en, ent, rst)
begin
if (rst ='0') then
ent <= (others => '0');
elsif (clk'event and elk = '1') then
if (en = '1') then
ent <= ent + '1';
end if;
end process;
count <= ent;
end behav;
```

b.   8-bit up counter with asynchronous load and reset

The following VHDL code describes an 8-bit up counter with asynchronous load and reset.

```vhdl
IEEE library;
use IEEE.std_logic_1164.all;
use IEEE.std_logic_unsigned.all;
use IEEE.std_logic_arith.all;
entity counter is
port (elk, reset, load: in StdJogic;
data: in std_logic_vector (7 downto 0);
count: out StdJogiC-Veetor (7 downto 0));
end counter;
architecture behave of counter is
signal count-i : std_logic_vector (7 downto 0);
begin
process (elk, reset)
begin
if (reset = '0') then
count-i <= (others => '0');
elsif (clk'event and elk = '1') then
if load = '1' then
count_i <= data;
else
count_i <= count_i + '1';
end if;
end if;
end process;
count <= countj;
end behave;
```

c.   N-bit up counter with load, count activation and asynchronous reset

The following VHDL code represents this VHDL code.

```vhdl
IEEE library;
use IEEE.std_logic_1164.all;
use IEEE.std_logic_unsigned.all;
use IEEE.std_logic_arith.all;
entity counter is
generic (width : integer := n);
port (data : in std_logic_vector (width-1 downto 0);
load, en, elk, rst : in StdJogic;
q : out std_logic_vector (width-1 downto 0));
end counter;
architecture behave of counter is
signal count: std_logic_vector (width-1 downto 0);
begin
process(clk, rst)
begin
if rst = '1' then
count <= (others => '0'};
elsif (clk'eventand elk = '1') then
if load = '1' then
count <= data;
elsif en = 'l' then
count <= count + '1';
end if;
end if;
end process;
q <= count;
end behave;
```

6.   Finite state machine :

A finite state machine (FSM) is a type of sequential circuit designed to pass through specific patterns of finite states in a predetermined sequential manner. There are two types of FSM, Mealy [11] and Moore [12].

Moore's FSM has outputs that are only a function of the current state. Mealy's FSM has outputs that are a function of the current state and the primary inputs. An FSM consists of 3 parts:

i.   Sequential register of current status :

The register, a set of n-bit flip-flops (state vector flip-flops) clocked by a single clock signal, is used to hold the state vector (current state or simply current state). The register, a set of n-bit flip-flops (state vector flip-flops) clocked by a single clock signal, is used to hold the state vector (current state or just state) of the FSM. An n-bit long state vector has 2^n possibilities, known as state encoding.

Often, not all 2^n combinations are needed, so those that are not used must be designed not to occur during normal operation. They must therefore be designed not to occur during normal operation. On the other hand, an m-state FSM requires at least l0g2(m) state vector flip-flops.

ii.   Combinatorial logic in the following state :

An FSM can only be in one state at any given time, and each active clock transition takes it from its initial state to its final state, as defined by next-state logic. The next state is a function of the inputs to the FSM and its current state.

iii.   Combined output logic :

The outputs are normally a function of the current state and possibly the primary inputs of the FSM (in the case of a Mealiy). Often, in a Moore FSM, you may want to derive the outputs from the next state, instead of the current state, when the FSM is running, instead of the current state, when the outputs are stored in the next state.

a. The Mealy FSM

Let's take this example of the finite state machine using Mealy's approach. Figure 14 illustrates it.

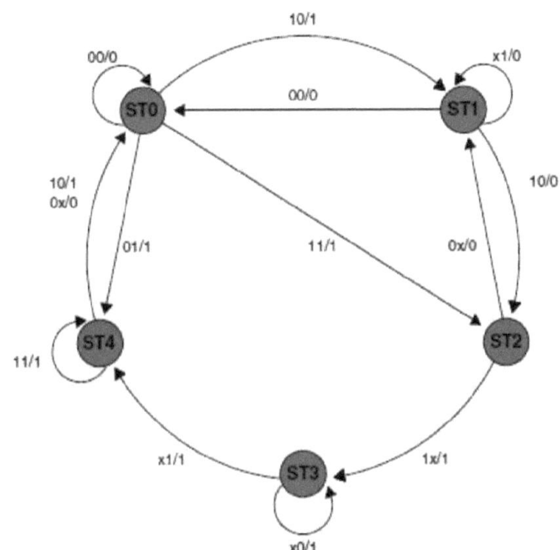

Figure 14 Mealy finite state machine

The VHDL code for the Mealy machine is as follows:

library ieee;

use ieee.std_logic_1164.all;

entity mealy **is**

port (clock, reset: **in** StdJogic;

data_out: **out** StdJogic;

datajn: **in** std_logic_vector (1 **downto** 0));

end mealy;

architecture behave **of** mealy **is**

type state_values **is** (st0, stl, st2, st3, st4);

signal pres_state, next_state: Stateyvalues;

begin

-      - FSM register

statereg: **process** (clock, reset)

begin

if (reset = '0') **then**

pres_state <= st0;

elsif (clock'eventand clock =T) **then**

33

```vhdl
pres_state <= next_state;
end if;
end process statereg;
-      - FSM combinational block
fsm: process (pres_state, datajn)
begin
case pres_state is
when st0 =>
case datajn is
when "00" => next_state <= st0;
when "01" => next_state <= st4;
when "10" => next_state <= stl;
when "11" => next_state <= st2;
when others => next_state <= (others <= 'x');
end case;
when stl =>
case datajn is
when "00" => next_state <= st0;
when "10" => next_state <= st2;
when others => next_state <= stl;
end case;
when st2 =>
case datajn is
when "00" => next_state <= stl;
when "01" => next_state <= stl;
when "10" => next_state <= st3;
when "11" => next_state <= st3;
when others => next_state <= (others <= 'x');
end case;
when st3 =>
case datajn is
when "01" => next_state <= st4;
when "11" => next_state <= st4;
when others => next_state <= st3;
end case;
when st4 =>
case datajn is
when "11" => next_state <= st4;
when others => next_state <= st0;
end case;
when others => next_state <= st0;
end case;
end process fsm;
-      - Mealy output definition using pres_state w/ datajn outputs: process (pres_state, datajn)
begin
```

```vhdl
case pres_state is
when st0 =>
case datajn is
when "00" => data_out<= '0';
when others => data_out <= '1';
end case;
when stl => data_out <= '0';
when st2 =>
case datajn is
when "00" => data_out<= '0';
when "01" => data_out<= '0';
when others => data_out <= '1';
end case;
when st3 => data_out <= '1';
when st4 =>
case datajn is
when "10" => data_out <= '1';
when "11" => data_out<= '1';
when others => data_out <= '0';
end case;
when others => data_out <= '0';
end case;
end process outputs;
end behave;
```

b. Moore's FSM

The code for Moore's machine is as follows:

```vhdl
library ieee;
use ieee.std_logic_1164.all;
entity moore is
port (clock, reset: in StdJogic;
data_out: out StdJogic;
datajn: in std_logic_vector (1 downto 0));
end moore;
architecture behave of moore is
type state_values is (st0, stl, st2, st3, st4);
signal pres_state, next_state: state_values;
begin
-- FSM register
statereg: process (clock, reset)
begin
if (reset = '0') then
pres_state <= st0;
elsif (clock = '1' and clock'event) then
pres_state <= next_state;
end if;
```

```vhdl
end process statereg;
-- FSM combinational block
fsm: process (pres_state, datajn)
begin
case pres_state is
when st0 =>
case datajn is
when "00" => next_state <= st0;
when "01" => next_state <= st4;
when "10" => next_state <= stl;
when "11" => next_state <= st2;
when others => next_state <= (others <= 'x');
end case;
when stl =>
case datajn is
when "00" => next_state <= st0;
when "10" => next_state <= st2;
when others => next_state <= stl;
end case;
when st2 =>
case datajn is
when "00" => next_state <= stl;
when "01" => next_state <= stl;
when "10" => next_state <= st3;
when "11" => next_state <= st3;
when others => next_state <= (others <= 'x');
end case;
when st3 =>
case datajn is
when "01" => next_state <= st4;
when "11" => next_state <= st4;
when others => next_state <= st3;
end case;
when st4 =>
case datajn is
when "11" => next_state <= st4;
when others => next_state <= st0;
end case;
when others => next_state <= st0;
end case;
end process fsm;
-- Moore output definition using pres_state only
outputs: process (pres_state)
begin
case pres_state is
```

when st0 => data_out <= '1';

when stl => data_out <= '0';

when st2 => data_out <= '1';

when st3 => data_out <= '0';

when st4 => data_out <= '1';

when others => data_out <= '0';

end case;

end process outputs;

end behave;

7. Conclusion

In this chapter, we have presented a few examples of VHDL exercises. We started with flip-flops, multiplexers, counters and finally finite state machines. In the appendix that follows, we will present an example of an embedded project using an FPGA-based platform.

CHAPTER 6

Practical application of VHDL

1. VHDL integration

The aim of this application is to integrate a VHDL block as a peripheral on the ML 507[13] and to test it.

The job involves :

- Take a VHDL multiplication block written and tested on ISE [14].
- Create a Microblaze-based architecture [15] on Xilinx EDK [16].
- Create and import the device on this architecture.

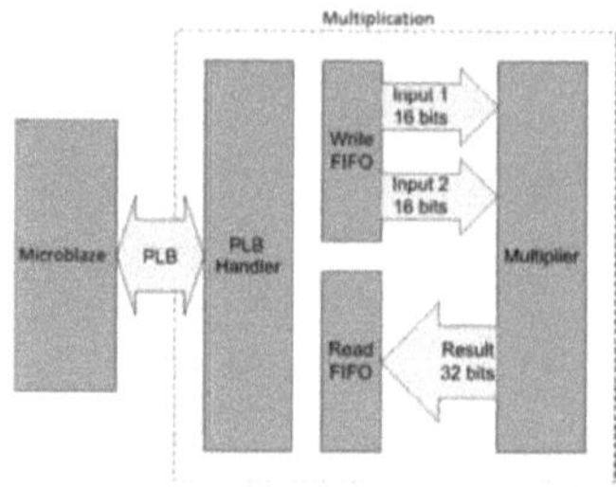

Multiplication has two 16-bit unsigned inputs and a 32-bit unsigned output.

We will use :

- A write operation on the 32-bit device. We have two inputs, each with a size of 16 bits. The bus is split into two parts, the lower 16 for the first variable and the upper 16 for the second variable.
- A 32-bit device read operation. The result of multiplying the two 16-bit inputs.

We are going to use a read and write on the FIFO [17] to interface with the software. In this way, the write FIFO device can be loaded according to the number of multiplications to be performed. The results can be sent to the read FIFO to be retrieved by the software.

a. Project creation

Follow the steps below:

1. Open XPS and select "Base System Builder wizard" then Ok.

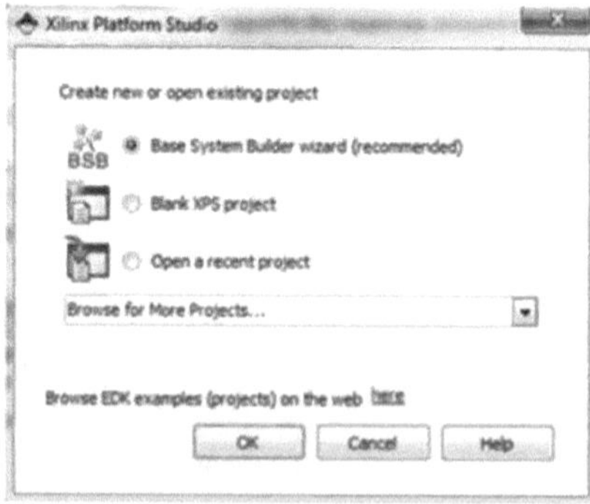

2. You will be asked to choose the folder in which to save the project. Click on "Browse" then create a new project. Name it system and click on "OK".

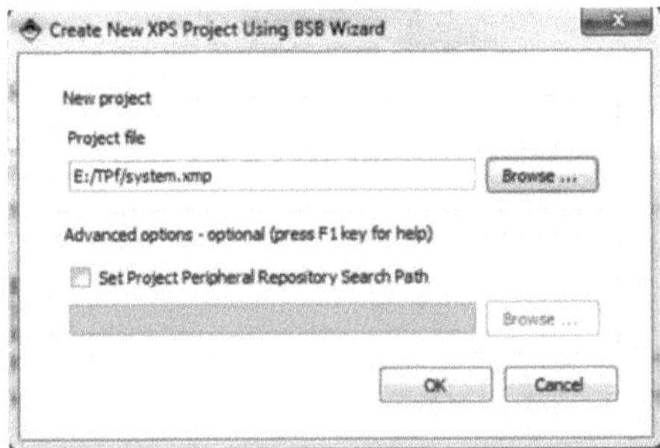

3. Select "I would like to create a new design" then click "Next".

4. In the "Select Board" menu, select "Xilinx" as the board vendor. Choose the ML 507 board with the existing FPGA characteristics

5. In the "Base system Builder" menu, select Single Processor System.
6. In the "Select Processor" page, you must choose between the PowerPC "hard" processor, or

the Microblaze "soft" processor. We will choose the Microblaze. Then click on "Next". Configure the Microblaze and select the clock frequency of 125MHz.

7. Keep the RS232 as well as the dlmb and ilmb

8. The result should be as follows.

9 The result is summarised in this figure

10. Click on "finish".
11. Select "Start using Platform Studio" then choose Ok

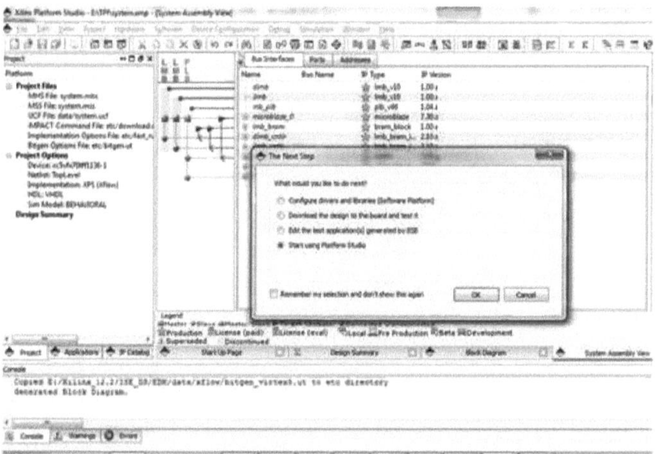

b. Creating a multiplication device

Follow the steps below to create a multiplication device.

1. Select "Hardware->Create or Import Peripheral" from the menu. Click on "Next".
2. Select "reate templates for a new peripheral" then click "next".

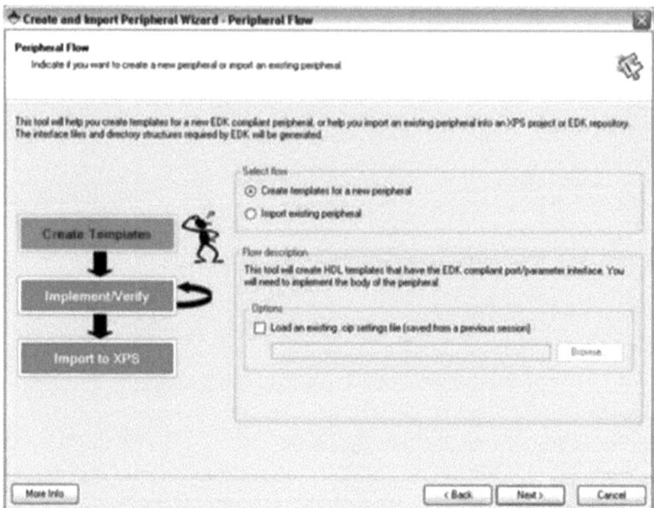

3. Select "To an XPS project". Click "Next".

3.   In the "Name and Version" page, type "my_multiplier" for the device name. Click "Next".

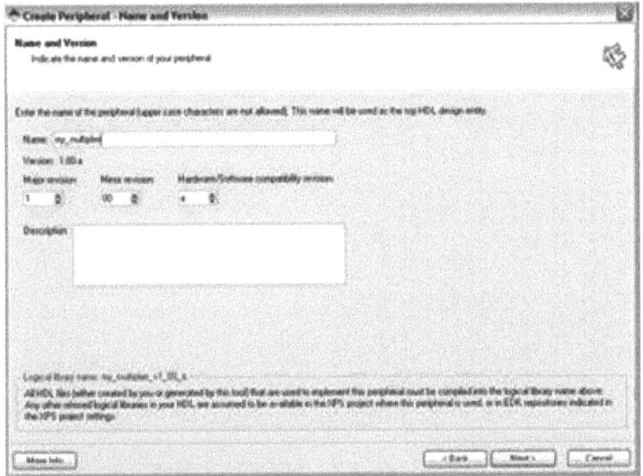

Select the "To an XPS" bus and click next.

6. In the "IPIF Services" page, the Peripheral Wizard can generate our VHDL template and include various data. Select "Read/Write FIFO" and "Include data phase timer" then click next

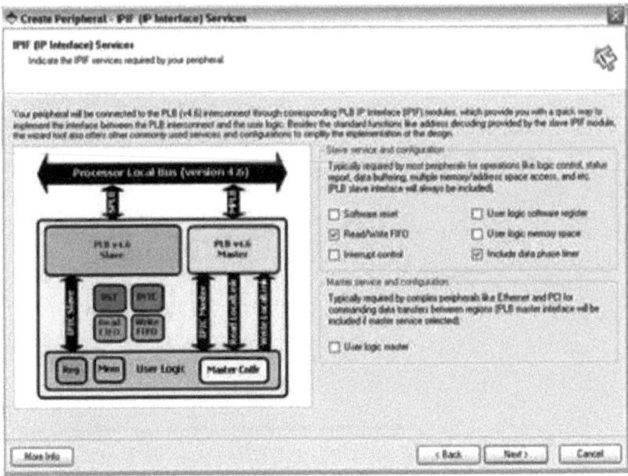

7. On the "Slave Interface" page, click "Next".

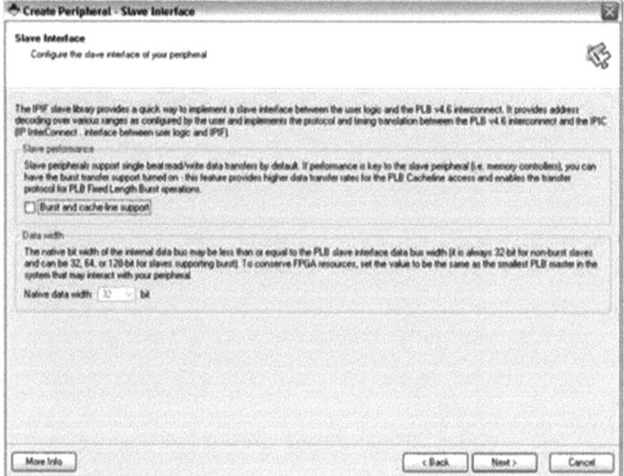

8. Keep the same data and choose a 512 KB FIFO.

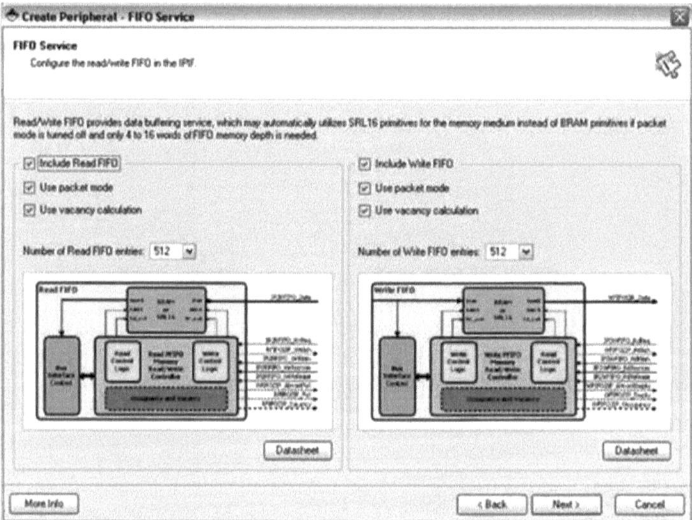

9. In the "IP Interconnect" page, keep the basic configuration and click on "Next".

10. In the "Peripheral Simulation Support" page, click "Next" without selecting anything.

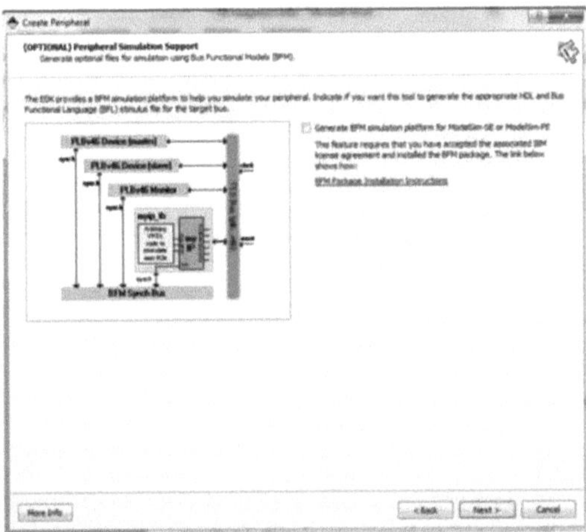

11. On the "Peripheral Implementation Support" page, select "Generate ISE and XST project files" and "Generate template driver files". Click "Next".

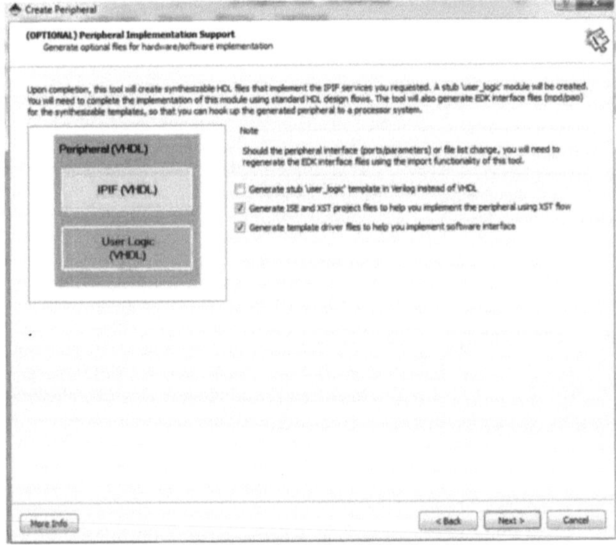

12. Click on "Finish". The skeleton of our accelerator is created.

c.   Creating the multiplier in VHDL

By following these steps, you can set up the multiplier to be used:

1.   Select "File->New". Write the VHDL code for the multiplication in it

2.   Copy the following code

```
libraryieee;
use ieee.std_logic_1164.all;
use ieee.std_logic_arith.all;
use ieee.std_logic_unsigned.all;
entity
multiplier is port(
```

```
elk : in StdJogic;
a : in std_logic_vector(15 downto
0); b : in std_logic_vector(15 downto 0); p : out std_logic_vector(31 downto 0]
J;
end multiply;
architecture IMP of multiplier is begin
process
(dk]
begin
if (clk'event and elk = '1'] then
p <= unsigned(a] * unsigned(b]; endif; end
process;
end IMP;
```

3.　Save the file with the title "multiply.vhd" in the "pcores\my_multiply_vl_00_a\ hdl\ vhdl" folder.

d.　Modifying the DTP file

The .pao file contains a list of all the files containing our device. We use this list when we call up the Peripheral Wizard in Import mode. As we have added the file ("multiplier.vhd"), it is important to include it in the .pao file.

1.　Select "File->0pen" and in the "pcores\my_multiplier_vl_00_a\data" folder. Choose the file "my_multiplier_v2_l_0.pao" then click on "Open".

2.　Add "lib my_multiplier_vl_OO_a multiply vhdl" after the lines :

lib my_multiplier_vl_OO_a UserJogic vhdl

lib my_multiplier_vl_OO_a my_multiplier vhdl

3.　Save file

Now that the addition has been successfully completed, it should be noted that each time a VHDL block is set up, a line must be added with its name and location in this file so that it can be pointed to.

e.　Device modification

Now that our code has been added to our device template, we'll instantiate our device and link it to our FIFO.

1.　Select "File->Open" from the project folder menu.

2.　Open the folder: "pcores\my_multiplier_vl_00_a\hdl\vhdl". It contains two source files describing our device. These are "my_multiplier.vhd" and "userjogic.vhd". The first represents the main of our device. It implements the interface to the OPB. The second file is where we will place our custom logic in order to manipulate our device.

3.　Open the "userjogic.vhd" file. We will instantiate the multiplier and connect it to the FIFO in read and write mode.

4.　Find the line "-USER signal declarations added here" and add the following lines just below it, componentmultiplier

```
port (
elk: in StdJogic;
a:    in std_logic_VECT0R(15 downto 0];
b:    in std_logic_VECT0R(15 downto 0];
p:    out std_logic_VECT0R(31 downto 0]];
end component;
```

5.　Find the line "-USER logic implementation added here" and add the following lines of code.

```
multiply_0 :
multiply port map (
clk=>Bus2IP_Clk,
a => WFIFO2IP_Data(16 to 31],
b => WFIF02IP_Data(0 to 15],
```

p => IP2RFIF0.Data];

6. Delete or comment on "IP2RFIF0_Data <= WFIF02IP_Data;"
7. Save and close the file.
f. Importing the Multiplier device

Now we're going to import the multiplication device.

1. Select "Hardware->Create or Import Peripheral" then click "Next".
2. Select "Import existing peripheral" then click next.

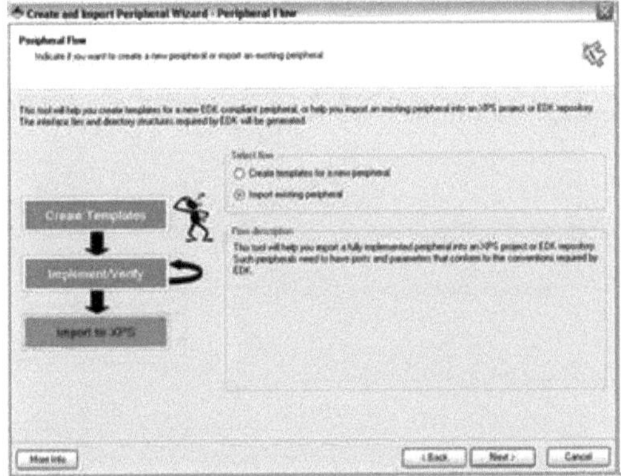

3. Select "To an XPS project", choose the project folder and click "Next".

4. Choose the file named "my_multiplier". Choose "Use version" and select the version created. Click on "Next". It will ask if you want to overwrite the existing version and you will select "Yes".

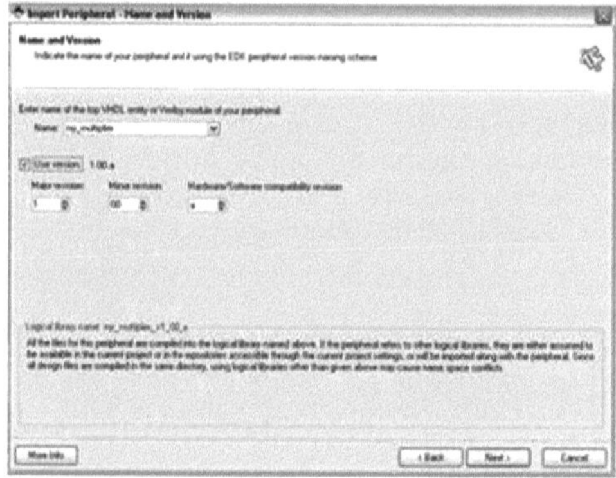

5. Now we are asked about the files that make up our peripheral. Tick 'HDL source files" and click "Next".

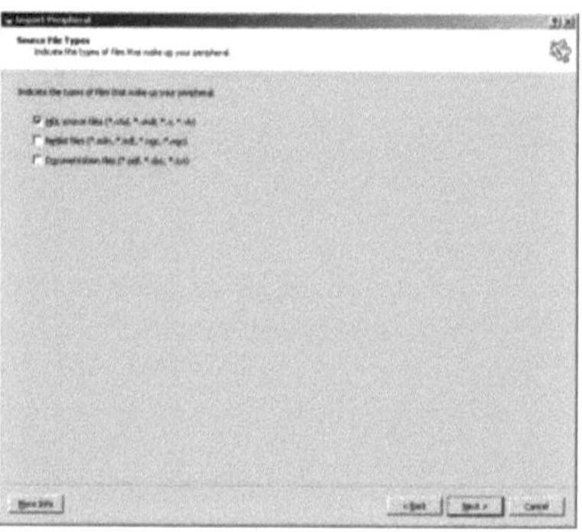

6. Select "Use existing Peripheral Analysis Order file (*.pao)" and click on "Browse". From project folder go to "pcores\my_multiplier_vl_00_a\data" and file "my_multiplier_v2_l_0.pao". Click on "Next".

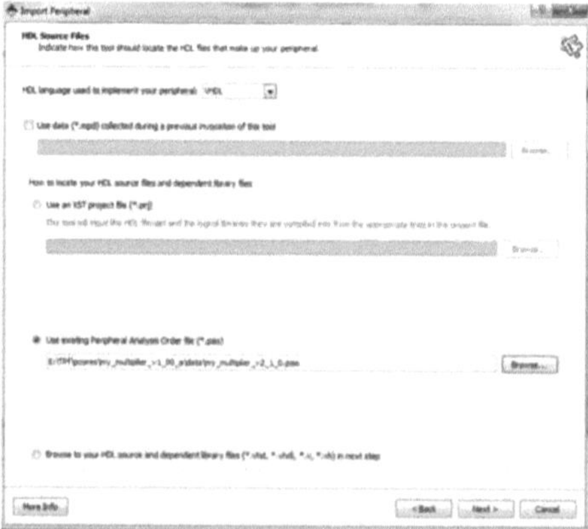

7. In the HDL analysis information page, you will find the file "multiplier.vhd. Click on "Next".

8. On the Bus Interfaces page, select "PLB Slave" and click "Next".

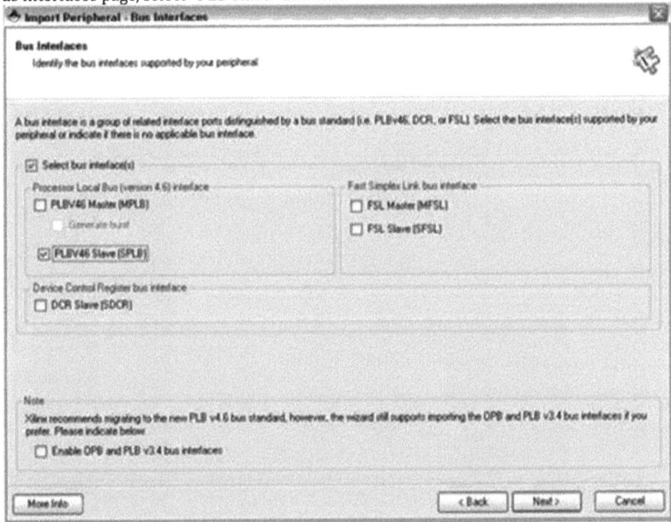

9. In SPLB: Portpage, click on "Next".
10. In SPLB:Parameter page, click on "Next".
11. On the "Parameter Attributes" page, click "Next".
12. On the "PortAttributes" page, click "Next".
13. Click on "Finish".

Our multiplier is now accessible from   "IP Catalog->Project Local peores
in the XPS interface.

g.   Create a device snapshot

Follow these steps to create an instance of the device in the project.

1.   From "IP Catalog" find "my_multiplier" IP in the "Project Repository" group. Right-click on the core and select "Add IP".

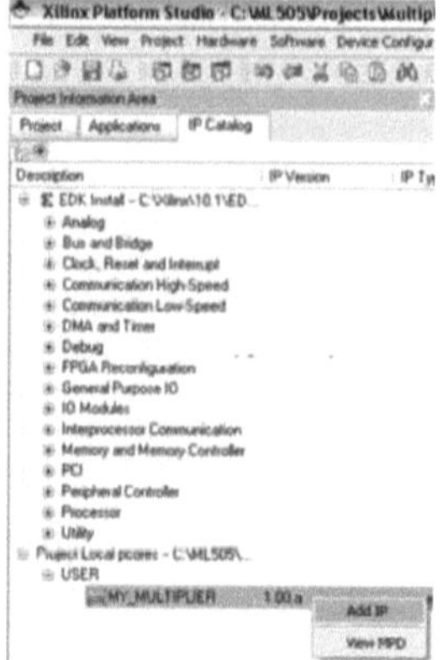

2. From "System Assembly View" using the "Bus Interface" connect "my_multiplier_0" to the PLB bus.

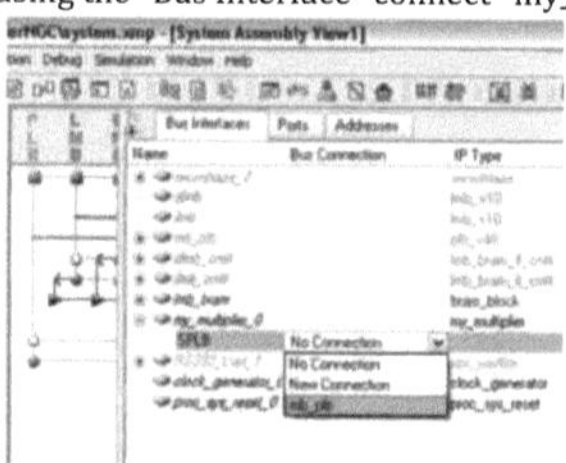

3. Click on "Addresses" filter. Change the size of "my_multiplier_0" to 64K. Then click on "Generate Addresses".

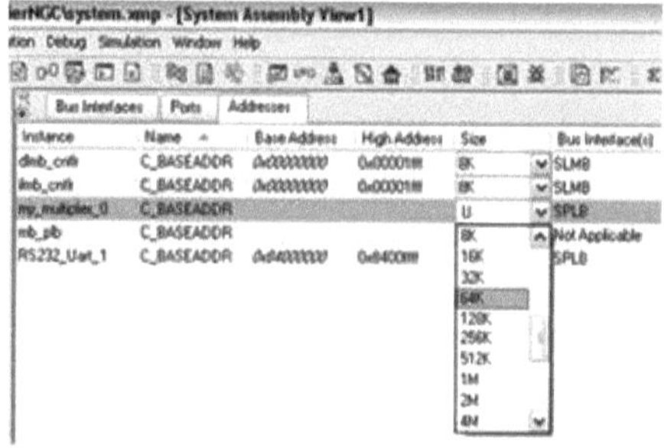

So the hardware design part is complete.

h. Modifying the Software application

We now need to modify our software application so that we can test it.

1. From the "Applications" tab, open "Sources" in the "Project: TestApp_Peripheral" tree. Open the source file "TestApp_Peripheral.c".

2. Replace the source code with the following code.

```
#include "xparameters.h"
#include "xbasic_types.h"
#include "xstatus.h"
#include "my_multiplier.h"
Xuint32 *baseaddr_p = (Xuint32 *)XPAR_MY_MULTIPLIER_0_BASEADDR;
intmain [void] { Xuint32 i; Xuint32 temp; Xuint32 baseaddr;
// Clear the screen
xiLprintf("%c[2J",27);
```

// Checkthattheperipheralexists XASSERT_NONVOID(baseaddr_p
!= XNULL]; baseaddr = (Xuint32] baseaddr_p;
xil_printf("Multiply Test\n\r"];
II Reset read and write packet FIFOs to initial state
MY_MULTIPLIER_mResetWriteFIFO(baseaddr];
MY_MULTIPLIER_mResetReadFIFO(baseaddr];
11 Push data to write packet FIFO for(i = 1; i <= 4; i++]{
temp = (i << 16] + i;
xil_printf("Wrote: 0x%08x \∏\r", temp];
MY.MULTIPLIERmWriteToFIFOtbaseaddr,0, temp);
}
// pop data out from read packet FIFO for(i = 0;i <
4; i++){
temp = MY_MULTIPLIER_mReadFromFIFO(baseaddr,0); xil_printf("Read: 0x%08x\n\r", temp);
}
// Reset the read and write FIFOs MY_MULTIPLIER_mResetWriteFIFO(baseaddr);
MY_MULTIPLIER_mResetReadFIFO(baseaddr);
xil_printf("End of test\n\n\r");
// Stayin an infinite loop while(l){
}
}
3.   Save and close the selected file
i.   Testing the Project
1.   Open the Hyperterminal and power up the ML 507.
2.   From the XPS software, select "Device Configuration->Download Bitstream". The result will be as follows:

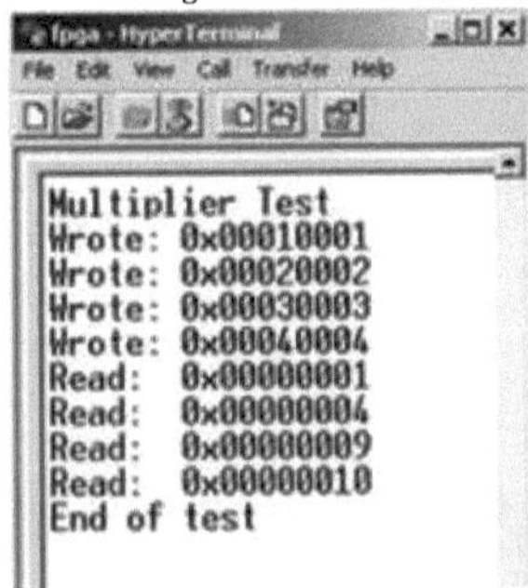

Multiplier Test Wrote: 0x00010001 Wrote: 0x00020002 Wrote: 0×00030003 Wrote: 0x00040004 Read: 0x00000001 Read: 0x00000004 Read : 0x00000009
Read: 0x00000010
End of test

j.   Shared memoryviinteraction

a. Introduction

In this lab, we will go through the steps required to create and run a microblaze-based dual-core system. Such a system requires the specification of both the hardware architecture and the software application that will be executed.

We are also going to introduce the concept :

-S Shared memory with synchronisation mechanisms

-S Mutex (Mutual exclusion) to ensure that a shared resource is not used simultaneously by both processors.

b. Working environment

S ML507 development board
S RS232 cable
S HyperTerminal or other terminal client
S Xilinx Platform Studio 12.1

c. Creating a project

♦   ♦♦ Navigate to Xilinx ISE Design Suite 12.1 → EDK → Xilinx Platform Studio After launching the tool, make sure Base System Builder is selected.

♦   ♦♦ Click Browse and specify where you want to create your project!

The path must not contain spaces C:/workshop/system.xmp The project will be saved as an .xmp file

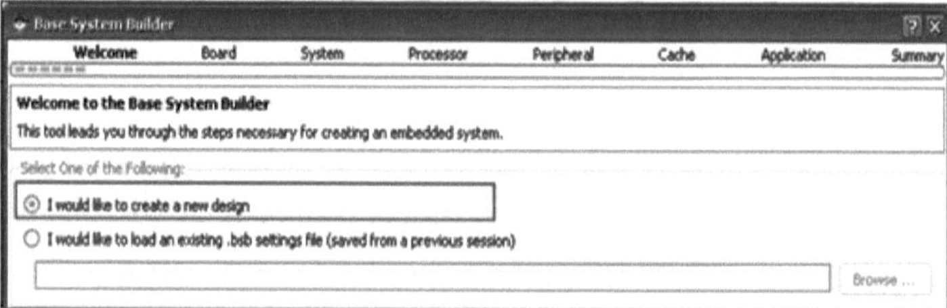

♦

♦   ♦♦ Create a new design

♦   ♦♦ Choose the target board for which you want to create the design: Virtex 5 ML507 Evaluation Platform.

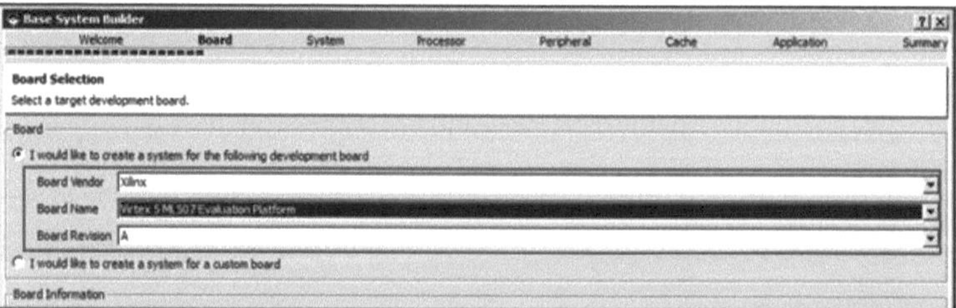

♦   ♦♦ You will be asked to choose between "Single Processor System" or "Dual- Processor System". In this lab, you will be developing a "Dual-Processor System".

♦   ♦♦ Choose :

S Microblaze as the type for both processors.

S 125 MHz as system clock frequency

S 64KB as local memory size

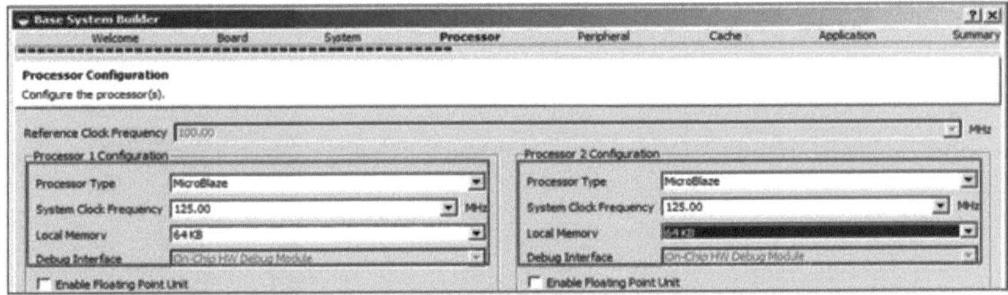

♦♦♦ The next step will allow you to add/remove devices to/from the system.

Configure the peripherals to obtain the following architecture:

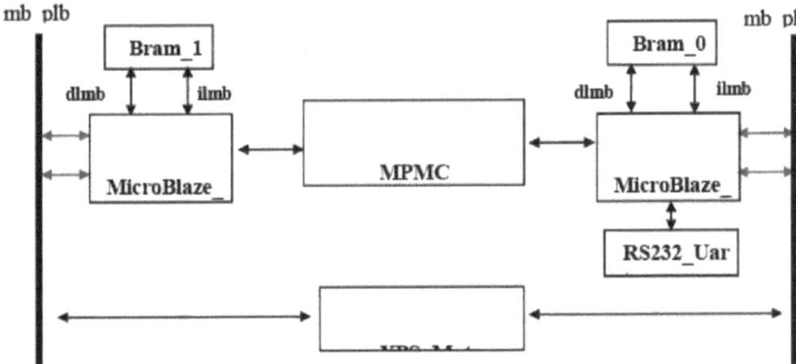

♦♦♦ Press Next until the "Summary" window appears, then Finish to generate your system.

Note: the frame on the left contains 3 tabs: *Project, Applications* and *IP Catalog.* It would be interesting to have a look at the MHS, MSS and UCF files located in Projecttab. The IP Catalog contains a collection of all the IPs that can be added to a system.

d.   Architecture generation

We are now ready to create the first part of the FPGA configuration, which is the description of the
! hardware architecture.

♦   ♦♦ Select Hardware → Generate netlist

This stage summarises the various IP blocks present in the system.

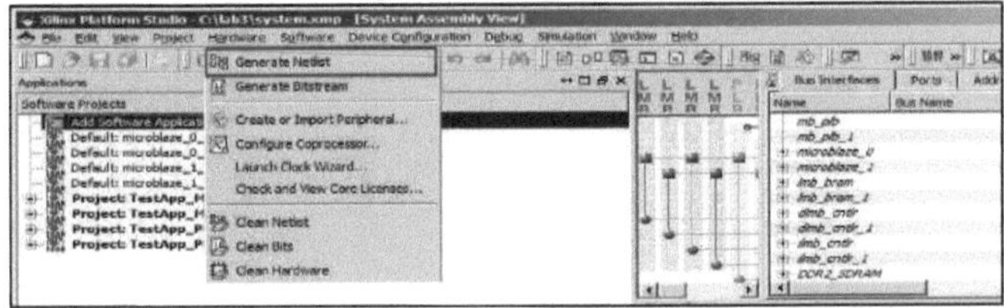

♦   ♦♦ After the synthesis stage, XPS must perform the mapping and placement and routing in order to obtain a bitstream .bit file present under implementation/system.bit.

Select Hardware → Generate bitstream

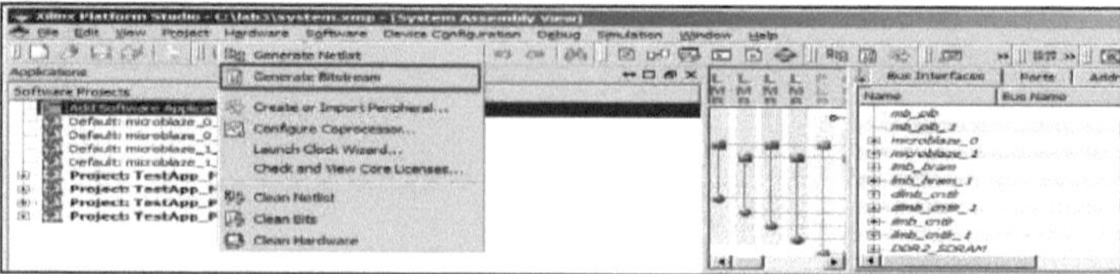

♦♦♦ UnderApplicationstab, LoadBRAMswithtwobootloops

The bootloop program must be used to occupy the processor until the application is loaded into memory.

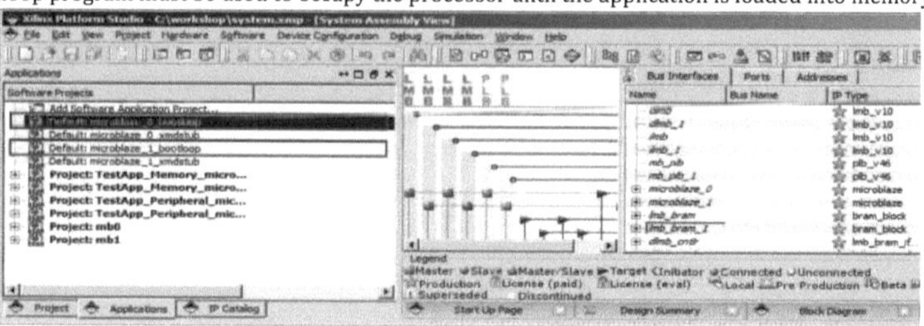

♦   ♦♦ The bitstream generated previously contains only hardware information.

To populate the software with the bitstream, we're going to do a bitstream update Select Device configuration → Update Bitstream

This step will combine the bitstream (system.bit) with the two bootloop elf files (microblaze_0.elf) and (microblaze_1.elf) to produce a file [download.bit] ready to be loaded into the FPGA.

♦   ♦♦ Select Device configuration → DownloadBitstream

e.   Software creation

The programme requested (producer/consumer]:

                 S microblaze_0 writes the value of i (i from 0 to 9]

S microblaze_1 reads this value and multiplies it by 10

S Each time microblaze_0 writes a value to memory, microblaze_1 reads it, multiplies it and displays it.

S the synchronisation mechanism is provided by Flags.

♦♦♦ Under Applications tab, double-click on Add Software Application Project

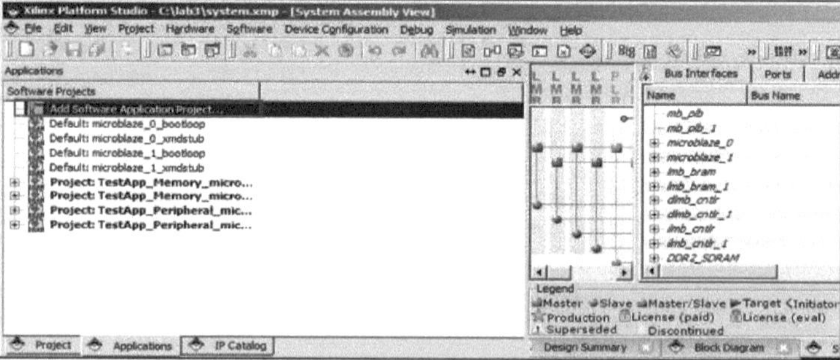

In the window that appears, enter the name of the project and the associated processor.
This step will be repeated twice: once for microblaze_0 and once for microblaze_l.

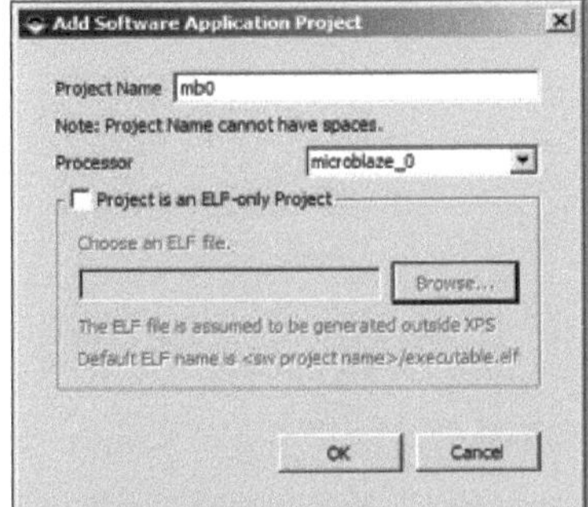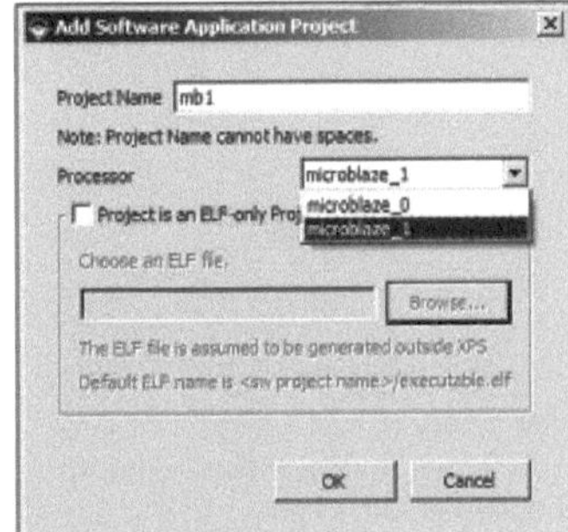

You'll notice that both projects have been created in the left-hand applications tab.
♦♦♦ Add a .c file to each project you create.
Right click on Sources → Add Existing file (the file will be supplied)

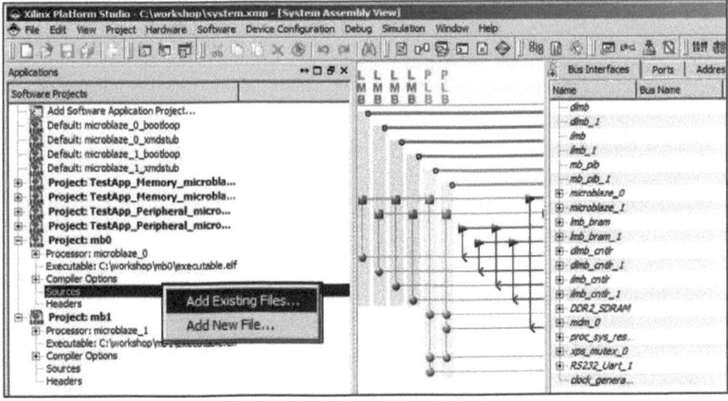

♦♦♦ Compile the two projects

f. Execution and display

The two processors communicate with the outside world via the UART.
The microblaze_0 uses the board's RS232_UART. As there is only one RS232 on the board and to visualise the output of microblaze_l, a JTAG_UART (mdm core) is available in each design.

FormicroblazeO
♦♦♦ Open RS-232 serial communication with the board usingTeraTeam

Formicroblazel ♦♦♦ Select Debug → launch XMD ♦♦♦ To connect to mdm_UART, type connect mdm -uart ♦♦♦
To open a TCP connection type terminal -jtag_uart_server 4321
Open a TCP/IP communication in Tera Term and set the port number to 4321.

This means that the two hyperterminals are open and each processor displays its output.

To run the project, you need to load the two applications onto the corresponding processors. To do this

♦♦♦ Open two XMD consoles

♦♦♦ Type the following commands for each processor:

S cd mb0

S dow executable.elf

S run

S cd mbl

S dow executable.elf

S run

```
C:\Xilinx\12.1\ISE_DS\EDK\bin\nt\xbash.exe
Connected to "mb" target. id = 0
Starting GDB server for "mb" target (id = 0) at TCP port no 1235
XMD% cd mb0
XMD% dow executable.elf
Processor Reset ..... DONE
Downloading Program -- executable.elf
        section, .vectors.reset: 0x00000000-0x00000003
        section, .vectors.sw_exception: 0x00000008-0x0000000b
        section, .vectors.interrupt: 0x00000010-0x00000013
        section, .vectors.hw_exception: 0x00000020-0x00000023
        section, .text: 0x00000050-0x00003d63
        section, .init: 0x00003d64-0x00003d87
        section, .fini: 0x00003d88-0x00003da3
        section, .ctors: 0x00003da4-0x00003dab
        section, .dtors: 0x00003dac-0x00003db3
        section, .rodata: 0x00003db4-0x0000438d
        section, .data: 0x00004390-0x000048c7
        section, .eh_frame: 0x000048c8-0x000048cb
        section, .jcr: 0x000048cc-0x000048cf
        section, .bss: 0x000048d0-0x0000494b
        section, .stack: 0x0000494c-0x00004d4f
Setting PC with Program Start Address 0x00000000
XMD% run
```

3. Example of synchronisation with IP Mutex when accessing a shared resource (RS232_UART)

The aim of this Lab B is to illustrate the use of XPS_Mutex to ensure synchronisation when accessing a shared resource. The shared resource in this example is the RS_232 interface. Both processors direct their STDOUT to the shared console. Without synchronisation, the console output will be garbled and useless. Therefore, each processor locks the XPS_Mutex before writing to the console and unlocks the Mutex when an output is made.

The most important peripheral in this architecture is the RS232 port, which is not an IP comprising a dual or multi-port, so this port will only be connected via a single PLB bus, meaning that only one processor can be debugged. So, to be able to display messages from both processors and debug them together, we need to add a PLB to PLB bridge that gives access to the second processor for the RS232 port, then the XPS_Mutex IP needs to synchronise these processors.

Procedure

❖ In IP Catalog tab, under

Bus and bridge Add

1'IP Plb46 to Plb46 Bridge

❖ Link this bridge to the rest of the architecture

J The Master port (MPLB) must be linked to microblaze_0 as the RS_232 belongs to it.

The Slave port (SPLB) must be linked to the microblaze_l

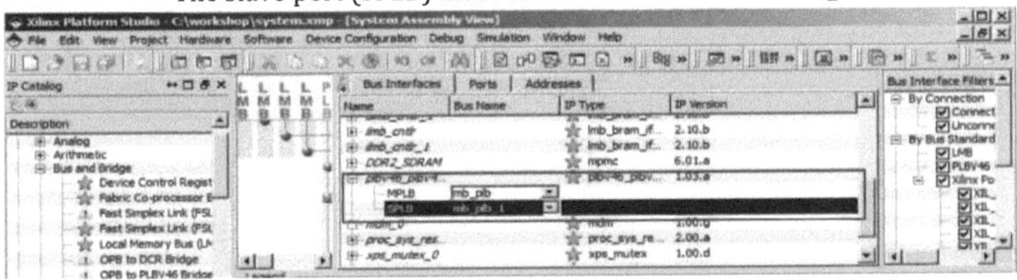

❖Under the Addresses tab

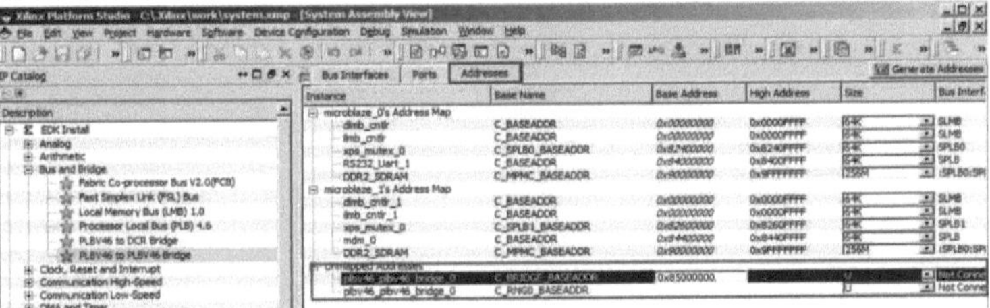

Associate with C_BRIDGE_BASEADDR

J Address 0x85000000

J 4K size

To give the second **processor** access to the RS_232 port, set the address of

C_Rango_BASEADDR to 64K.

❖ Generate lebitstream

❖ The program to be implemented is the one described above.

J Modify the code using Mutex for synchronisation.

J Check that STDIN and STDOUT on the second processor are assigned to the RS 232 interface.

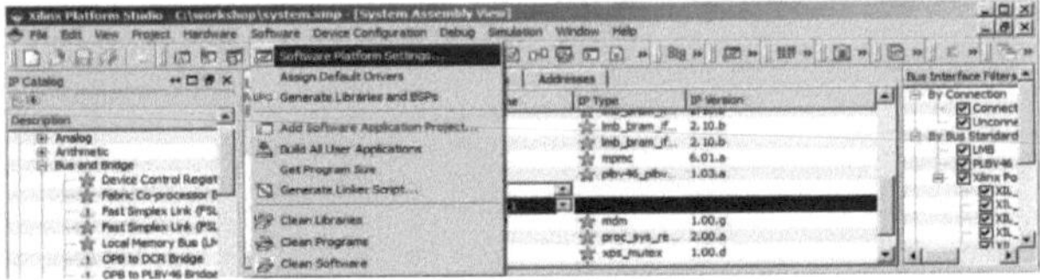

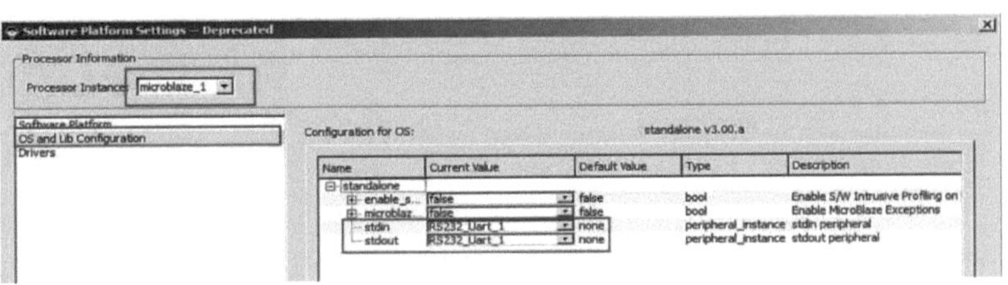

J Compile your projects.

❖ Run both applications through XMD at the same time
❖ Check the output of both processors (the display on a single HyperTerminalj.

References

[1]   C. Alexandre, "Digital design in VHDL", Conservatoire National des Arts et Métiers, FIP-CPI 2017-2018

[2]   https://www.ieee.org/, visited on 01/12/2023

[3]   IEEE Standard VHDL Language Reference Manual, in *IEEEStd 1076-2002 (Revision of IEEE Std 1076, 2002 Edn)*, vol. no., pp.1-308, 17 May 2002, doi: 10.1109/IEEESTD.2002.93614.

[4]   IEEE Standard VHDL Language Reference Manual," in *ANSI/IEEE Std 1076-1993*, vol. no., pp.1-288, 6 June 1994, doi: 10.1109/IEEESTD.1994.121433.

[5]   D. Biederman, "An overview on writing a VHDL testbench," *Proceedings The Twenty-Ninth Southeastern Symposium on System Theory*, Cookeville, TN, USA, 1997, pp. 384-388, doi: 10.1109/SSST.1997.581677.

[6]   Pong P. Chu, RTL Hardware Design UsingVHDL: Coding for Efficiency, Portability, andScalability, B017S2I996, Publisher: JohnWiley&SonsInc

[7]   https://www.intel.com/content/www/us/en/software-kit/750368/modelsim- intel-fpgas-standard-edition-software-version-18-l.html, visited on 05/01/2024

[8]   https://www.hdlworks.com/hdl_corner/vhdl_ref/VHDLContents/PortMap.htm, 05/01/2024

[9]   Actel HDL Coding, Style Guide

[10] R. P. Ribas, A. I. Reis and A. Ivanov, "Performance and functional test of flipflops using ring oscillator structure," *2011 IEEE 6th International Design and Test Workshop (IDT)*,   Beirut, Lebanon, 2011, pp. 42-47, doi:
10.1109/IDT.2011.6123099.

[11] https://www.emse.fr/~dutertre/documents/machines_a_etats.pdf

[12] http://wiki.polymtl.ca/nano/fr/images/e/e2/INF1500H10Cours8.pdf

[13] https://www.xilinx.com/support/documentation-navigation/boards-and-kits/virtex-5/ml507.html, visited on 15/07/2022

[14] https://www.xilinx.com/products/design-tools/ise-design-suite.html, visited on 18/07/2022

[15] https://www.xilinx.com/products/design-tools/microblaze.html, visited on 18/07/2022

[16] https://www.xilinx.com/products/design-tools/platform.html, visited on 18/07/2022

[17] https://docs.xilinx.eom/v/u/13.l-English/pg057-fifo-generator, visited on 18/07/2022

[18] https://www.xilinx.com/products/design-tools/xps.html, visited on 20/07/2022

I want morebooks!

Buy your books fast and straightforward online - at one of world's fastest growing online book stores! Environmentally sound due to Print-on-Demand technologies.

Buy your books online at
www.morebooks.shop

Kaufen Sie Ihre Bücher schnell und unkompliziert online – auf einer der am schnellsten wachsenden Buchhandelsplattformen weltweit! Dank Print-On-Demand umwelt- und ressourcenschonend produziert.

Bücher schneller online kaufen
www.morebooks.shop

info@omniscriptum.com
www.omniscriptum.com

Printed by Books on Demand GmbH, Norderstedt / Germany